DK EYEWITNESS

T0063900

TOP 10
SCOTLAND

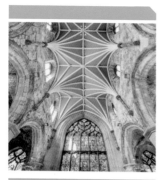

Top 10 Scotland Highlights

The Top 10 of Everything

CONTENTS

Scotland Area by Area

Streetsmart

Within each Top 10 list in this book, no hierarchy of quality or popularity is implied. All 10 are, in the editor's opinion, of roughly equal merit.

Title page, front cover and spine Old Sligachan Bridge on the Isle of Skye
Back cover, clockwise from top left *Jacobite Steam Train at Glenfinnan; Isle of Harris; Calton Hill, Edinburgh; Isle of Skye; University of Glasgow*

The rapid rate at which the world is changing is constantly keeping the DK Eyewitness team on our toes. While we've worked hard to ensure that this edition of Scotland is accurate and up-to-date, we know that opening hours alter, standards shift, prices fluctuate, places close and new ones pop up in their stead. So, if you notice we've got something wrong or left something out, we want to hear about it. Please get in touch at **travelguides@dk.com**

Welcome to
Scotland

Shimmering lochs, silent glens, romantic castles, remote islands, vibrant festivals, drams of whisky and rounds of golf. The birthplace of "Rabbie" Burns and Harry Potter is a proud nation, and no wonder, Scotland has fuelled the passions of artists, writers and adventurers for centuries. With DK Eyewitness Top 10 Scotland, it's your turn to be inspired.

It may be small, but few countries can match Scotland's mix of scenic splendour and cultural heritage. What could be more romantic than crossing the sea to the **Isle of Skye**, more moving than seeing the site of the **Glencoe** massacre or more exciting than experiencing the world-famous **Edinburgh International Festival**? And what could be more thrilling than watching ospreys in the **Cairngorms National Park**, monster-spotting for "Nessie" on **Loch Ness** or exploring fairy-tale **Glamis Castle** – supposedly one of the most haunted places in Britain?

Scotland has long attracted thrill-seekers, who come to "bag" a Munro or to hike the **West Highland Way**. Yet its gentler activities are prized too, such as strolling among the colourful plants of **Inverewe Gardens** or spotting **Moray Firth Dolphins** off the coast. Its cultural attractions are equally varied: Impressionist paintings and exquisite architecture in Glasgow; Edinburgh's castle, museums and galleries; Victorian industry in **New Lanark's** historic streets and Viking graffiti at **Maeshowe** on Orkney.

Whether you're visiting for a weekend or a week, our Top 10 guide brings together the best of everything Scotland has to offer, from mysterious **Rosslyn Chapel** to mighty **Ben Nevis**. The guide has useful tips throughout, from seeking out what's free to finding places off the beaten track, plus 11 easy-to-follow itineraries, designed to tie together a clutch of sights in a short space of time. Add inspiring photography and detailed maps, and you've got the essential pocket-sized travel companion. **Enjoy the book, and enjoy Scotland.**

Clockwise from top: Portree harbour in Skye, Scottish dancers, Greyfriars Bobby in Edinburgh, Rua Reidh Lighthouse near Gairloch on the northwest coast, the Falkirk Wheel, Highland cattle, Scottish Parliament in Edinburgh

Exploring Scotland

Scotland offers wild landscapes, ancient castles and bustling cities. To help make the most of your stay and get a flavour for this fascinating country, here are ideas for a two-day and a seven-day Scottish jaunt.

The Queen's Gallery, at the Palace of Holyroodhouse, exhibits works from the Royal Collection.

Forth Bridge, a UNESCO World Heritage Site, is a cantilever railway bridge near Edinburgh.

Two Days in Scotland

Day ❶
MORNING
Start in Edinburgh with the historic **Royal Mile** *(see pp14–15)* and tour the Palace of Holyroodhouse.
AFTERNOON
Choose between the **National Museum of Scotland** *(see pp18–19)* or the **Scottish National Gallery** *(see pp16–17)*. Head to New Town to shop at the St James Quarter shopping centre *(see p79)*, then take in the fabulous city views from **Calton Hill** *(see p76)*.

Day ❷
MORNING
Drive to romantic **Linlithgow Palace** *(see p86)*, then continue to the site of the battle of **Bannockburn** *(see p103)*.
AFTERNOON
Take in dramatic **Stirling Castle** *(see p103)* and visit the Wallace Monument. Return via the charming streets of **Culross** *(see p91)* and majestic **Forth Bridge** *(see p94)*.

Key
— Two-day itinerary
— Seven-day itinerary

Seven Days in Scotland

Day ❶
As day 1 of Two Days in Scotland.

Day ❷
MORNING
Cross the Forth to visit historic **Scone Palace** *(see p92)* before lunching by the silvery Tay in Perth.
AFTERNOON
Head for Loch of the Lowes, near **Dunkeld** *(see p94)*, to view the ospreys (Apr–Aug). Then continue through Pitlochry to the picturesque gorge at Killiecrankie.

Day ❸
MORNING
Ride the wonderful **Strathspey Steam Railway** *(see p35)*, then warm your cockles at a distillery on Speyside's Malt Whisky Trail.

Eilean Donan Castle is one of Scotland's iconic sites, located on an island where three lochs converge.

AFTERNOON
Spot **Moray Firth dolphins** *(see p112)* from the shore of Spey Bay. Stay overnight in **Inverness** *(see p117)*.

Day ❹
MORNING
Explore the bleak **Culloden Battlefield** *(see p117)*, then keep your eyes peeled on a "monster" cruise on the famous Loch Ness.
AFTERNOON
Watch boats on the Caledonian canal at **Fort Augustus** *(see p29)*. Bear west to **Eilean Donan Castle** *(see p118)*, then cross the bridge from Kyle of Lochalsh to **Isle of Skye** *(see pp26–7)*.

Day ❺
MORNING
Start early and visit **Dunvegan Castle** *(see p26)*, ancestral home of the Clan Macleod and purportedly the oldest inhabited castle of Scotland.

AFTERNOON
Take a boat trip from Elgol to **Loch Coruisk** *(see p26)*. Leave the Isle of Skye from Armadale in time to catch the last ferry to Mallaig.

Day ❻
MORNING
Admire the **Glenfinnan Monument** *(see p118)* and viaduct, and continue to sombre **Glencoe** *(see pp30–31)*.
AFTERNOON
Take the High Road to **Loch Lomond** *(see p103)*, stopping in pretty Luss for a break, and arriving in **Glasgow** *(see pp96–101)* in time for dinner.

Day ❼
MORNING
Spend the morning at **Kelvingrove Art Gallery and Museum** *(see pp20–21)* or the **Riverside Museum** *(see pp22–3)*.
AFTERNOON
Down the Ayrshire coast find **Culzean Castle** *(see pp32–3)* and the **Robert Burns Birthplace Museum** *(see p85)*.

Top 10 Scotland Highlights

Rib-vaulted ceiling and stained-glass windows
of St Giles' Cathedral, Edinburgh

🔟 Scotland Highlights

Scotland is renowned for its overwhelming abundance of natural beauty, as well as its array of impressive castles, signposts of the country's long and turbulent past. It also has a rich culture, being home to countless museums and art galleries – all filled with treasures – and one of the world's most iconic festivals. Here's a distillation of Scotland's best.

Edinburgh Castle ①

Presiding over the nation's capital, the castle is Scotland's pre-eminent sight, a truly inspirational historical and cultural landmark (see pp12–13).

② Scottish National Gallery

The gallery's internationally significant collection ranges from early Renaissance masterpieces to works by Rembrandt, Ramsay and Raeburn (see pp16–17).

③ National Museum of Scotland

The main museum has one of Scotland's great eclectic collections. The modern wing takes on Scotland from prehistory to the 20th century (see pp18–19).

Kelvingrove Art Gallery and Museum ④

Inside its grand Spanish Baroque-style shell, Scotland's premier museum and art gallery houses one of Europe's great civic art collections (see pp20–21).

⑤ Riverside Museum

With its dramatic saw-toothed roof, this is one of Glasgow's most striking museums. Filled with interactive exhibits, it is dedicated to transport through the ages; there are over 3,000 objects on display, including an old carriage from the Glasgow subway and models of ships built on the Clyde (see pp22–3).

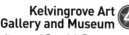

6 Isle of Skye

Skye is an island of romantic tales and the pursuit of royalty, of strange landscapes and formidable mountain ranges, of castle strongholds and religious communities *(see pp26–7)*.

7 Loch Ness and the Great Glen

The Great Glen is Scotland's deepest cut, a swathe that splits the land in two. A course of water runs through this great valley, forming notorious Loch Ness *(see pp28–9)*.

8 Glencoe

Described by Dickens as the "burial ground of a race of giants", there is indeed something ominous about this raw terrain, site of a 1692 massacre *(see pp30–31)*.

9 Culzean Castle

Standing on a windswept clifftop, Culzean is a lavish 18th-century castle. Admire Robert Adam's striking Neo-Classical interior, complete with a dramatic oval staircase *(see pp32–3)*.

10 The Cairngorms

This region offers truly spectacular views. Bird lovers, walkers and winter sports enthusiasts praying for snow all head to the woodlands, rivers, lochs and mountains of the Cairngorms, the highest landmass in Great Britain. From ospreys to Arctic flowers, it's all here to discover *(see pp34–5)*.

🔟⭐ Edinburgh Castle

Dominating the city's skyline since the 12th century, this castle is a national icon and, deservedly, one of the country's most popular visitor attractions. Din Eidyn, "the stronghold of Eidyn", from which Edinburgh takes its name, was the vital possession in Scotland's wars. Varying roles as royal palace, barracks, prison and parliament have all helped shape this castle, home to the Scottish crown jewels and the fabled Stone of Destiny.

1 Gatehouse and Portcullis Gate

The gatehouse was built in 1886–8 more for its looks than functionality. The two bronze statues are of William Wallace and Robert the Bruce (see p103). The original entrance was via the formidable Portcullis Gate of around 1574.

2 Great Hall

The outstanding feature of this hall (below) is the hammer-beam roof supported on projecting stone corbels. Take time to study all the enchanting little carvings. Constructed around 1500, this is Scotland's oldest wooden roof and probably its most magnificent.

The imposing façade of Edinburgh Castle

3 Argyle Battery

The castle's northern defence offers spectacular views. Don't miss the One O'Clock Gun, fired here every day except Sunday from a great 25-pounder cannon.

4 Crown Jewels and the Stone of Destiny

The UK's oldest crown jewels have lain here since about 1615. However, the fabled Stone of Destiny has been here only since 1996.

5 Scottish National War Memorial

The National War Memorial (right) lists all of Scotland's war dead since 1914. Exterior carvings include a phoenix, symbol of the surviving spirit.

7 St Margaret's Chapel

This tiny, charmingly simple building is the oldest structure surviving from the medieval castle. Probably built by David I (1124–53) in honour of his sanctified mother, it is still used today, and contains some wonderful stained glass (left).

8 Royal Palace

Here in 1566, in a small panelled chamber, Mary Queen of Scots gave birth to James VI, the first king to rule both Scotland and England.

9 Governor's House

This elegant house is beautifully proportioned. It can only be viewed from the outside, as it is still reserved for ceremonial use.

10 Mons Meg

A cannon (below) of awesome proportions now sits outside St Margaret's Chapel. Built in Belgium in 1449, it could fire a 150-kg (330-lb) stone ball over 2 miles (3.5 km) – cutting-edge technology in the Middle Ages.

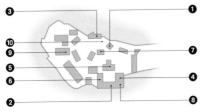

6 Prison Vaults

During the 18th and 19th centuries, the castle's vaults were used to hold French prisoners of war. Their graffiti can still be seen, as can the objects they made, such as bone dyes for forging banknotes.

Plan of the Castle

STONE OF DESTINY

According to the mythology that surrounds the Stone, this is the very rock that Jacob used as a pillow when he dreamed of angels ascending to heaven (Genesis 28). For centuries it was kept in Scone Palace, near Perth (see p92), and used as the coronation throne for Scottish kings until Edward I invaded in 1296 and carried the Stone back to England. For 700 years it was kept under the throne in Westminster Abbey, until it was returned to Scotland in 1996.

NEED TO KNOW

MAP M4 ■ Castle Hill, Edinburgh, EH1 2NG ■ (0131) 225 9846 ■ www.edinburgh castle.scot

Open Apr–Sep: 9:30am–6pm daily (Oct–Mar: to 5pm); last adm 1 hour before closing; closed Christmas Day & Boxing Day; tours every 30 min

Adm £19.50; concessions £16; children £11.50

■ Book tickets online for reduced prices and guaranteed entry time.

■ The official tours are witty and informative. You can also take a multilingual audio tour, proceeding in whatever order takes your fancy.

■ Although a large variety of food can be found on the Royal Mile just outside the castle, choice at the castle itself is limited to either the Tea Rooms or the Redcoat Café (see p77).

The Royal Mile

John Knox's House on Edinburgh's Royal Mile

1 John Knox's House
MAP P3 ■ 43–5 High St ■ (0131) 556 9579 ■ Open 10am–6pm Mon–Sat (Jul & Aug: from noon Sun) ■ Adm ■ www.scottishstorytellingcentre.com

The best-known little house in Edinburgh, with its quaint steps up from the street, is now part of the Scottish Storytelling Centre. It was the home of Scotland's fiery religious reformer, John Knox, in 1599. Worth squeezing into for its antiquity alone.

2 Writers' Museum
MAP N3 ■ Lady Stair's Close ■ (0131) 529 4901 ■ Open 10am–5pm daily ■ www.edinburgh museums.org.uk

Occupying Lady Stair's House (built in 1622) and set in a charming court-yard, this is the place to learn about the three great Scottish writers,

THE ROYAL MILE

The city's most historic street formed the main thoroughfare of medieval Edinburgh, linking the castle to Holyroodhouse. Thronged with street performers during the Festival (see p68), it is a hub of entertainment year-round. Don't miss the narrow closes off the main street.

Robert Burns, Sir Walter Scott and Robert Louis Stevenson, through portraits, manuscripts and personal possessions (see p78).

3 St Giles' Cathedral
MAP N4 ■ High St ■ (0131) 225 9442 ■ Open 10am–6pm Mon–Fri, 10am–5pm Sat, 1–5pm Sun ■ Donation ■ www.stgilescathedral. org.uk

This building (see p78) has been a landmark and a marvel since 1160. Look for the bagpiping angel (near the entrance), the exhilarating rib-vaulted ceiling of the Thistle Chapel and those ancient tatty flags. There is a self-service café and a shop here as well.

4 Scottish Storytelling Centre
MAP P3 ■ 43–5 High St ■ (0131) 556 9579 ■ Open 10am–6pm Mon–Sat (Jul & Aug: from noon Sun) ■ www. scottishstorytellingcentre.com

A theatre with a wide range of entertainment, but the insider thing to do here is enquire about the local storytellers. They hold meetings in the café on the last Friday of every month, where anyone can enjoy the craic (good times). Nothing flamboyant, but real local culture.

5 Museum of Childhood

MAP P3 ▪ 42 High St ▪ (0131) 529 4142 ▪ Open 10am–5pm daily ▪ www.edinburghmuseums.org.uk

Teddy bears, rocking horses, toy soldiers and castor oil – childhood memories come rippling back in the minds of adult visitors. But today's children find the Museum of Childhood just as enthralling, as they discover what amused their older relatives long ago; there's also an excellent play space for children.

6 Historic and Ghostly Tours

Mercat Tours: (0131) 225 5445; www.mercattours.com ▪ Auld Reekie Tours: (0131) 557 4700; www.auldreekietours.com ▪ Cadies & Witchery Tours: (0131) 225 6745; www.witchery tours.com ▪ City of Edinburgh Tours: (0131) 220 6868; www. cityofedinburghtours.com

The Witchery Tour

A fascinating tour can be taken of Mary King's Close (see p78), a medieval street sealed up in 1646 after its inhabitants died of the plague. Alternatively, choose an adrenalin-pumping ghost tour – evenings are best.

7 Scottish Parliament

MAP R3 ▪ Canongate ▪ (0131) 348 5200 ▪ Open 10am–5pm Mon-Sat, public hols & all days Parliament is in recess ▪ www.parliament.scot

Spanish architect Enric Mirrales's controversial design of "upturned boats" won the competition for a landmark building for the new Scottish Parliament. Higher up the Mile is the old Parliament House.

8 Museum of Edinburgh

MAP Q3 ▪ 142 Canongate ▪ (0131) 529 4143 ▪ Open 10am–5pm daily ▪ www.edinburgh museums.org.uk

A medieval house, this museum has a specialist local collection. A maze of rooms comprises primitive axe heads, Roman coins and all manner of historical finds gathered from the street since the Neolithic Age.

Map of the Royal Mile

9 The Palace of Holyroodhouse

MAP R3 ▪ Royal Mile ▪ (0303) 123 7306 ▪ Open Apr–Oct: 9:30am–6pm daily (Nov–Mar: to 4:30pm daily); last adm 1 hour 15 min before closing (call to check for closing times) ▪ Adm ▪ www.rct.uk

The royal residence (see p76) was known for love and murder in the time of Mary Queen of Scots. The state rooms are used by the current Queen. Climb nearby Arthur's Seat in Holyrood Park for views.

10 Camera Obscura

MAP M4 ▪ Castlehill ▪ (0131) 226 3709 ▪ Times vary, check website ▪ Adm ▪ www.camera-obscura.co.uk

This historic observatory has a roving mirror that projects a 360° panorama of Edinburgh, so it is a great place to start exploring the city. In the World of Illusions, meanwhile, you can immerse yourself in over 100 exhibits that are sure to amaze and entertain you. Afterwards, head to the rooftop terrace to enjoy and take snaps of the spectacular views of the city.

The vortex tunnel at Camera Obscura

★ Scottish National Gallery

A striking Neo-Classical building midway along Edinburgh's Princes Street, the Scottish National Gallery defies you to miss it and is widely regarded as one of the finest smaller galleries in the world. The collection is a manageable concentration of excellence, including works by the greatest names in Western art – Raphael, Titian, El Greco, Rembrandt and Monet, to name but a few. There's also a comrehensive array of Scottish masterpieces by the likes of Raeburn, Wilkie, McTaggart and more.

1 Seven Sacraments
The seven works depicting the rites of Christianity evoke grand theatricality; they are considered the finest pieces by Nicolas Poussin, founder of French Classical painting.

2 An Old Woman Cooking Eggs
Velázquez's creation of mood through strong contrast was unprecedented in Spain when he produced this startling work (below) in 1618.

3 Lady Agnew of Lochnaw
The lady's languid pose and direct gaze in this portrait (above) caused a stir in 1892, launching her as a society beauty and giving John Singer Sargent cult status among Edwardian-era portrait painters.

4 The Virgin Adoring the Sleeping Christ Child
The painting's brilliant range of tones has now been revealed following careful restoration. An unusual Botticelli work for having been painted on canvas and not wood.

5 Rev Robert Walker Skating on Duddingston Loch
One of the most celebrated paintings by a Scottish painter, the fun-loving minister depicted by Henry Raeburn is known to have been a member of the prestigious Edinburgh Skating Club.

6 Dutch Collection
The pick of the best from the Dutch collection must include Rembrandt's world-weary *Self-Portrait Aged 51*, though *A Woman in Bed* also has an impressive depth of character. Dutch paintings in the galleries include works by Frans Hals, such as his lively, naturalistic *Portrait of Verdonck*.

7 Italian Renaissance Paintings

Works by Leonardo da Vinci and Raphael stand out here. Leonardo's *Madonna of the Yarnwinder* depicts the Christ child holding a spindle shaped like a cross, while Titian's *The Three Ages of Man* reminds us of everlasting love.

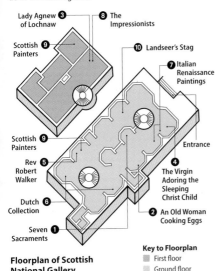

Floorplan of Scottish National Gallery

- ❸ Lady Agnew of Lochnaw
- ❽ The Impressionists
- ❾ Scottish Painters
- ❿ Landseer's Stag
- ❼ Italian Renaissance Paintings
- ❾ Scottish Painters
- Entrance
- ❺ Rev Robert Walker
- ❻ Dutch Collection
- ❹ The Virgin Adoring the Sleeping Christ Child
- ❷ An Old Woman Cooking Eggs
- ❶ Seven Sacraments

Key to Floorplan
- First floor
- Ground floor

8 The Impressionists

You can find works by Impressionists such as Monet and Cezanne here, as well as Gauguin's *Vision of the Sermon* (Jacob Wrestling with the Angel) and Van Gogh's *Orchard in Blossom* **(below)**.

9 Scottish Painters

The collection includes superb portraits by Ramsay, Raeburn and Guthrie, *Pitlessie Fair* by Sir David Wilkie aged 16, and *Saint Bride* by John Duncan. Check to see which works are being displayed during restoration.

10 Landseer's Stag

Sir Edwin Landseer's *Monarch of the Glen* is known to be one of the most famous of all Victorian British paintings. It depicts a magnificent stag in a Highland setting.

TOP 10 ⭐ National Museum of Scotland

The best and rarest of Scotland's antiquities have been brought together in this treasure trove occupying connected buildings on Edinburgh's Chambers Street. Both buildings maintain separate identities: the older 19th-century building concentrates on international artifacts, while the modern sandstone wing is dedicated to the story of Scotland and its people.

1 Lewis Chess Pieces

These enchanting ivory figures – an anxious king, a pious bishop, glum warriors – were made by Viking invaders in the 12th century.

2 Monymusk Reliquary

Reliquaries were containers used for storing holy relics. The Monymusk Reliquary is connected to St Columba and Robert the Bruce, a key figure of Bannockburn *(see p38)*. It dates back to the 8th century and, although it's tiny, the craftsmanship is exceptional. It is one of the most prized possessions of the musuem.

3 The Maiden

This is a grisly relic to put a shiver down your spine. The Maiden was a Scottish beheading machine, which predated the French guillotine, with a weighted blade that descended from on high. It was used to behead more than 150 of those condemned in Edinburgh between 1564 and 1710, including its inventor.

Display of Vivienne Westwood's tartan suit

4 Art, Design and Fashion

This splendid gallery showcases innovation in applied arts, fashion and design. Among the many exhibits, the most eye-catching are six Wedgwood plates by Sir Eduardo Paolozzi from the 1970s and a tartan suit by Vivienne Westwood (1993).

5 Bonnie Prince Charlie's Canteen

Find the fugitive Prince's *(see p27)* cutlery, corkscrew, bottles, cup and condiments set here, and picture him in the wild with his lustrous travelling canteen.

6 Ancient Egypt Rediscovered

Covering more than 4,000 years of Egyptian history, this gallery showcases iconic objects **(left)** from this ancient culture. Exhibits include a complete royal burial group as well as exquisite gold jewellery.

7 Natural History

Dinosaur skeletons and stuffed animals cascade down from the ceiling, producing spectacular visual results that almost bring them to life.

8 Dolly the Sheep

An ordinary-looking sheep **(left)** that's anything but that. As the world's first cloned mammal, Dolly was a scientific marvel.

The Buildings 9

The National Museum first opened as the Royal Museum in 1866 and has been a city landmark ever since. Its cavernous interior and marvellous roof create an extraordinary feeling of light and space. The sandstone wing **(right)** has been heralded as one of the most important constructions in postwar Scotland.

Floorplan of National Museum of Scotland

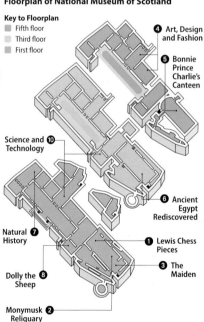

Key to Floorplan
- Fifth floor
- Third floor
- First floor

4 Art, Design and Fashion
5 Bonnie Prince Charlie's Canteen
Science and Technology 10
6 Ancient Egypt Rediscovered
Natural History 7
1 Lewis Chess Pieces
3 The Maiden
Dolly the Sheep 8
Monymusk Reliquary 2

ORIENTATION

Centred on the vast foyer, the older part of the National Museum is spread over three floors. Wandering the many halls can be confusing, so pick up a floor plan or ask the staff for help. The layout of the sandstone wing, accessed by the Tower Entrance, is more straightforward. The roof terrace of the Scottish Galleries offers spectacular views of the city.

NEED TO KNOW

MAP N4 ■ Chambers St, Edinburgh, EH1 1JF
■ (0300) 123 6789
■ www.nms.ac.uk

Open 10am–5pm daily

■ There are temporary exhibits on display thoughout the year.

■ Check timings and schedule for free guided tours at the main desk.

■ The museum's rooftop Tower Restaurant has fantastic views.

10 Science and Technology

Dolly the Sheep is just one of Scotland's modern scientific achievements. This gallery looks at some of the country's other genetic research along with its Nobel Prize-winning work on pharmaceuticals. One particularly futuristic exhibit looks at the production of state-of-the-art body implants and prosthetic limbs, developed by local company Touch Bionics.

TOP 10 ⭐ Kelvingrove Art Gallery and Museum

Scotland's most visited collection comprises some 8,000 works of international significance. The collection takes in worldwide ancient cultures, as well as European and Scottish art across the centuries, and provides insights into the development of Glasgow from medieval times through to its cultural transformation in the 19th to 21st centuries, including the 2014 Commonwealth Games, when the city stole the show with its hospitality and sense of fun. There is also a quirky playfulness in Kelvingrove's contrasting displays.

1 Miss Cranston's Tearoom

Between 1900 and 1921 the venerable Charles Rennie Mackintosh (1868–1928) was the sole designer for Catherine Cranston's tearoom empire. These beautiful interiors are of both artistic and social significance.

2 Sir Roger

Kelvingrove's most popular inhabitant is Sir Roger, a stuffed Asian elephant. Sir Roger spent the late 19th century in a travelling circus – Bostock and Wombwell's Menagerie – before being moved to a Glasgow zoo in 1897. It was here that the elephant lived out his final days.

West Court, Kelvingrove Art Gallery and Museum

3 Spitfire

The Spitfire LA198, 602 City of Glasgow Squadron, hangs dramatically from the ceiling of the West Court (above), soaring above the bodies of stuffed giraffes and wild cats. It is recognized as the best-restored warplane of its kind in the UK.

4 Old Willie the Village Worthy

A leading figure in the group of young, rebellious Scottish artists known as the Glasgow Boys, James Guthrie (1859–1930) produced internationally significant work in the late 19th century. The unsentimental *Old Willie the Village Worthy* (left), is one of Guthrie's finest realist portraits.

5 A Man in Armour

This fine painting by Rembrandt – a highlight of the museum's renowned collection of 17th-century Dutch and Flemish masters – is a bold depiction of a young man, probably Alexander the Great, weighed down by his armour. Kelvingrove curators voted it their favourite piece. The work dates back to the mid-17th century.

6 Paddle Canoe

This fascinating paddle canoe, which was carved from a single piece of wood, is one of the few remaining artifacts from a forgotten world. It dates back to Scotland's Bronze Age (c 2500–800 BC) and would have been used by early people living in crannogs, or loch dwellings.

Floorplan of Kelvingrove Art Gallery and Museum

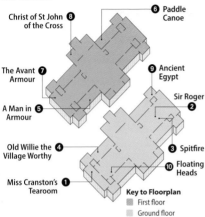

- **8** Christ of St John of the Cross
- **6** Paddle Canoe
- **7** The Avant Armour
- **9** Ancient Egypt
- **5** A Man in Armour
- **2** Sir Roger
- **4** Old Willie the Village Worthy
- **3** Spitfire
- **10** Floating Heads
- **1** Miss Cranston's Tearoom

Key to Floorplan
- First floor
- Ground floor

7 The Avant Armour

This artwork and tool of war is one of the oldest near-complete suits of armour in the world and is still in almost perfect condition. Made in Milan, a centre of armour-making, in around 1440, it is a key piece in Kelvingrove's collection.

8 Christ of St John of the Cross

Salvador Dalí's surrealist painting was first displayed in 1952. The unusual angle of the crucifixion attracted admiration, criticism and controversy, which was typical of Dalí.

9 Ancient Egypt

Wonders abound in the Ancient Egypt gallery, including mummies and tombs. The coffin and mummy of Egyptian lady Ankhesnefer date back to 610 BC. Her mummified body has remained in the coffin since her funeral and burial approximately 2,500 years ago.

10 Floating Heads

This literally head-turning art installation (left) by Scottish artist Sophie Cave features over 50 suspended, sculpted heads, each bearing a different expression ranging from laughter to despair. Placed in the main foyer, the installation is the first thing you will encounter upon entering the Art Gallery and Museum.

Riverside Museum

A former "European Museum of the Year" winner, this stunning £74 million building on the banks of the Clyde is devoted to transport, technology and leisure. In addition to its extraordinary collection of trains and trams, boats and bikes, cars, and even skateboards, the museum also considers and takes a look at the social impact transport has had on the city of Glasgow. You can easily spend a few hours at this terrific museum which is interactive throughout.

1 The Building
Take time to stroll outside and admire the building (above) designed by the acclaimed late architect Zaha Hadid. The museum sits on the site of a former shipyard. The jagged roof is striking, and the interior is free of supports to accommodate several large exhibits.

2 South African Locomotive
Built in Glasgow in 1945, this enormous locomotive spent more than 40 years crossing South Africa. It is the largest object in the collection and one of a number of restored trains.

3 All Things Bike
Bicycles and motorbikes on display include Graham Obree's one-hour world record breaking bike and the world's oldest pedal bike. Suspended from the ceiling is a model velodrome.

4 Recreated Streets
There are three recreated streets that take you back to the Glasgow of the past. Most atmospheric is the cobbled 19th-century street with its shops, pub and an interactive photographer's studio.

THE CLYDE

"Glasgow made the Clyde and the Clyde made Glasgow." After trade in sugar and tobacco expanded in the 18th century, engineers deepened the Clyde, which eventually allowed boats to dock in the city itself, rather than unload their cargoes downriver. International trade developed, shipbuilding became a major industry and Glasgow grew into the "second city" of the British empire.

Map of Riverside Museum

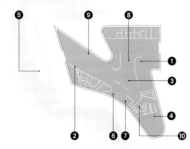

NEED TO KNOW

MAP Y2 ■ 100 Pointhouse Place, Glasgow G3 8RS

■ (0141) 287 2720

■ www.glasgowlife. org.uk/museums/ riverside

Open 10am–5pm Mon–Thu & Sat (from 11am Fri & Sun)

The Tall Ship: Pointhouse Quay; (0141) 357 3699; open 10am–4pm daily

■ The café on the ground floor has great views of the Clyde; in warmer weather you can dine outside on the terrace.

■ There are free guided tours on most days and fun family quiz sheets. Ask at the reception.

⑤ The Tall Ship

Moored on the Clyde outside the museum, the *Glenlee* (right) is one of the five Clyde-built sailing ships that remain afloat. Built in the 19th century, it circumnavigated the globe four times. Tour the ship, and even see the captain's cabin.

⑥ The Italian Caffè

Glasgow's Italian community has been well established in the city since the 19th century. They have founded a number of much-loved cafés in the city and along the Ayrshire coast. This re-creation of a typical 1930s Italian café has chequered floors and wooden booths.

⑦ The Subway

Step into a model section of the Glasgow subway and climb aboard a carriage from an old underground train, where you can watch a short film starring 50 actors and volunteers dressed in costumes from the 1940s.

⑧ Glasgow Tram

Glasgow's trams achieved iconic status and were an important part of the city's culture until 1962. You can step inside this original street-car (right) and discover stories associated with the trams and city life.

⑨ Wall of Cars

There aren't many places where you can see the first Hillman Imp, an Argyll motor and a pristine Strathclyde Police Ford Granada. A wide variety of old and new cars (left) are on display, many of which are reminders of Glasgow's famous motor industry.

⑩ Clyde-Built Ships

Glasgow was once a world-famous centre of shipbuilding and the museum has over 160 models of Clyde-built ships, including luxury liners and warships. Models on display include the *Cutty Sark*, the *Lusitania* and the *Queen Mary*. There is also a World War I warship decorated with distinctive "dazzle" camouflage.

🔟 ⭐ Isle of Skye

The product of violent geographical upheavals, the "Misty Isle" is justly famed for its towering, ragged mountains and wild coastline. Add to these a colourful patchwork of crofts (farms), waterfalls, an exceptional whisky distillery, a castle linked to the fairy-tale world and the historical romance of Bonnie Prince Charlie, and you find on Skye all the ingredients that best symbolize the Scottish Highlands.

Quiraing and the Old Man of Storr ④

A fantastic region of cliffs and pinnacles, one rocky outcrop (right) gaining the name the Old Man of Storr.

⑤ The Cuillins

This awesome range rises straight out of the sea to almost 1,000 m (3,300 ft). The Black Cuillins are a challenge even to seasoned climbers, but the Red Cuillins are an easier prospect for walkers.

① Loch Coruisk

The boat from Elgol passes seal colonies to reach this lovely loch (above), trapped in a bowl beneath the Cuillins – a prized view awaits.

⑥ Armadale Castle Gardens and Museum of the Isles

Beautiful coastal gardens surrounding the ruined castle of Clan MacDonald, with an historical archive.

② Coral Beach, Claigan

The pure white sand and turquoise waters of this picture-perfect beach make it appear deceptively tropical, especially on sunny summer days.

⑦ Dunvegan Castle

Dunvegan (left) was home to the chiefs of Clan MacLeod for 1,000 years. Find the Fairy Flag, which, it is said, can rally the "little people" to protect the clan.

Portree ③

Portree is Skye's mini capital, with some excellent shops and a delightful harbour lined with colourful buildings (right). Sailing races and Highland Games are big events in summer.

Previous pages Quiraing, Isle of Skye

**Map of
Isle of Skye**

FLORA MACDONALD

"Bonnie Prince Charlie" was pursued relentlessly by government troops following his defeat at Culloden. He escaped to Skye disguised as a maid-servant thanks to the courageous Flora MacDonald. She was imprisoned for this act. On her release she emigrated to America, but later returned to Skye, where she died in 1790. One of the prince's bedsheets was her burial shroud.

8 Talisker Distillery
The so-called "lava of the Cuillins" is produced at Skye's original whisky distillery, where visitors are welcomed onto a friendly tour.

9 Island of Raasay
Its beauty often overlooked, Raasay offers land-based activities and watersports at its Outdoor Centre, or you can climb Dun Caan, the highest point on the island, for stunning views.

10 Skye Museum of Island Life
Delightfully evocative, this reconstruction of thatched cottages **(below)**, or "blackhouses" (blackened by fire smoke), turns the years back a century or more.

NEED TO KNOW

MAP D2

Armadale Castle: (01471) 844 305; open Apr–Oct: daily; Mar & Nov: Mon–Fri; adm adults £9, concessions £7.50, children £5

Dunvegan Castle: (01470) 521 206; open Apr–mid-Oct: daily; adm adults £14, concessions £11, children £9

Talisker Distillery, Carbost: (01478) 614 308; open Mar–Oct: 9:30am–5pm Mon–Sat (from 10am Sun); Nov–Feb: 10am–4:30pm daily; tours £15

Skye Museum of Island Life: (01470) 552206; open Easter–Sep: 9:30am–5pm

Mon–Sat; adm adults £4, children 50p; www.skye museum.co.uk

Misty Isle Boat Trips, Elgol: (01471) 866288

■ **The Sligachan Hotel** *(IV47 8SW; (01478) 650 204; www.sligachan.co. uk),* 5 km (3 miles) west of Sconser, offers great bar meals and stunning views.

TOP 10 ⭐ Loch Ness and the Great Glen

A geological rift once split the land from coast to coast, dividing Scotland in two. Glaciers deepened the trench and the result today is a long glen of steep-sided, wooded mountains and dark, mysterious lochs. Castles and forts abound, bearing witness to the Great Glen's strategic importance and enhancing its dramatic grandeur with intrigue and nostalgia. And the legendary Loch Ness Monster, elusive but irrepressible, still attracts significant interest.

1 Caledonian Canal

The canal **(below)** is an outstanding feat of engineering by Thomas Telford, connecting lochs Ness, Oich, Lochy and Linnhe. Watch boats glide past at Fort Augustus.

2 Loch Lochy

A path on this loch's **(below)** northern shore is now part of the Great Glen Walk and cycleway. Look out for the wonderful Cia Aig waterfall on the road to Loch Arkaig.

3 Fort William

Close to Glencoe and at the foot of Britain's highest mountain, Ben Nevis (1,345 m / 4,413 ft), this seaside town provides an ideal base for walkers. Almost every direction offers enticing terrain. The less active can scale Aonach Mor on the Nevis Range ski gondola or take the Jacobite Steam Train to Mallaig.

4 Great Glen Water Park

A sensitively landscaped centre among trees on Loch Oich, the smallest and most secluded in the glen. You can go canoeing, kayaking, canyoning, rock climbing or shoot the rapids on a raft.

5 Glen Affric

A lovely forest road leads to this renowned beauty spot. From here, a two-day hike can take you to the west coast.

TALES OF NESSIE

First recorded by St Aiden in the 7th century, "Nessie" pops up time and again. Despite many hoaxes and faked photographs, there's still a body of sonar and photographic evidence to support the existence of large creatures here, and scientific opinion remains open. To decide for yourself, visit one of the Loch Ness Monster information centres in Drumnadrochit, which present the evidence.

6 Inverness

The "Capital of the Highlands", Inverness is a bustling shopping centre set below a pink Victorian castle. The battlefield of Culloden *(see p38)* is nearby and the visitor centre there revives this sad and poignant event.

7 Urquhart Castle

Magnificently situated on the edge of Loch Ness, these ruins **(below)** were formerly one of Scotland's largest castles. A fine tower house still stands, and the views from the top are well worth the climb. The state-of-the-art visitor centre displays an array of medieval artifacts.

Map of Loch Ness and the Great Glen

8 Fort George

Built in the aftermath of Culloden on a sandy promontory in the Moray Firth, Fort George **(below)** is the mightiest artillery fortification in Britain. It is still in use as a barracks today, yet remarkably has only ever undergone minor modifications.

9 Loch Ness

Almost 230 m (750 ft) deep and 37 km (23 miles) long, Loch Ness is Scotland's largest waterbody. Flanked by mountains, castle and abbey ruins, and charming villages, Loch Ness is worthy of its fame. Jacobite lake cruises start from the north road along its bank. Other cruises leave from Inverness.

NEED TO KNOW

MAP E3–D4

Jacobite Steam Train: open mid-May–Oct: Mon–Fri (mid-Jun–mid-Sep: daily); www.west coastrailways.co.uk

Urquhart Castle: (01456) 450 551; open daily; adm adults £12, concessions £9.60, children £7.20

Fort George: (01667) 462 834; open daily; adm adults £9.50, concessions £7.50, children £5.50

Loch Ness Centre and Exhibition, Drumnadrochit: open daily; adm adults £8.95, concessions £7.95, children £4.95; www.lochness.com

Jacobite Cruises (Canal and Loch Ness): open daily; www.jacobite.co.uk

■ Admission to most sights is free for Historic Environment Scotland Members *(check www. historicenvironment.scot/ membership)*

10 Fort Augustus

Fort Augustus is a delightful village situated on Loch Ness. Take a stroll along the canal and the loch shore to watch yachts and canal cruisers along the Great Glen.

TOP 10 ⭐ Glencoe

Nowhere else is the traveller confronted so abruptly by the arresting impact of Scotland's mountains. The road twists below the towering bulk of these characterful peaks, sometimes dark and louring, sometimes light and enticing. This ancient and celebrated pass is also imbued with history: cattle rustling, clan feuds and – most notoriously – the "Massacre of Glencoe" in 1692. In summer the area is a favourite haunt of walkers and climbers; in winter it is one of the leading ski resorts in the country.

① Glencoe Visitor Centre

This centre possesses a superb exhibition and audiovisual presentation – allow an hour to take it all in. A satellite weather report for the area is regularly updated; useful for walkers.

THE MASSACRE OF GLENCOE

Having signed an oath of submission to William III in 1692, albeit five days late, the MacDonald clan generously entertained and billeted 130 government soldiers in their homes for 10 days. The soldiers then slaughtered their hosts, leaving 38 dead. As much as the brutality of the massacre, it was the utter breach of trust that shocked the nation.

② Signal Rock, Glencoe Memorial and Forest Walk

A series of forest trails leads to the Signal Rock lookout (**left**), where the MacDonalds *(see p43)* would light fires to send messages to clan members.

③ Invercoe Loch Walk and Pap of Glencoe

A particularly beautiful loch (**above**), especially in May, when its rhododendrons are in full bloom. Behind looms the distinctive Pap of Glencoe peak, affording panoramic views.

④ Views of the Three Sisters

By a bend in the main road and next to a roaring waterfall, visitors will find a rocky knoll known as "The Study", which is a fine viewpoint for this trio of similarly profiled sibling mountains (**below**).

Map of Glencoe

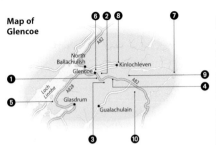

10 Glencoe Ski Centre

Among the most popular of Scotland's five ski resorts **(below)**. All the gear is available for hire in winter, and the terrain is ideal for snow thrills.

7 Rannoch Moor

A beautiful but boggy wilderness, best seen from a window on the Fort William to Tyndrum train.

8 Ice Factor

This exciting activity centre offers a wide range of indoor aerial adventures as well as outdoor courses. Their 12-m- (39-ft-) tall ice climbing wall is made of ice and snow, which weighs up to 500 tonnes. They feature a rock climbing wall too. Activities here are overlooked by professional instructors.

5 Castle Stalker

A dreamlike castle **(below)**, alas not open to visitors but still magical to see, rising from an island that seems barely big enough to contain it.

6 Loch Leven

The charming drive round this loch is punctuated by modest villages. Discover Glencoe's diverting museum and Kinlochleven's visitor centre that tells the story of 80 years of aluminium production here.

9 Devil's Staircase

A tortuous section of the West Highland Way walk *(see p52)*, offering views to Rannoch Moor and Black Mount. The footpath continues to Kinlochleven for an even greater challenge.

NEED TO KNOW

MAP E3

Glencoe Visitor Centre: (01855) 811 307; open late Mar–Oct: 9am–6pm daily; Nov–Feb: 10am–4pm daily; adm £4 (free for National Trust for Scotland (NTS) members); www.nts.org.uk

Glencoe Folk Museum: (01855) 811 664; open Apr–Oct: 10am–4:30pm Tue–Sat; adm £3; www.glencoemuseum.com

Ice Factor: (01855) 831 100; open 9am–6pm daily; adm 1 hr sample session adult £30, junior £25 (12 yrs or above), 2.5 hr instructed ice climb £48; www.ice-factor.co.uk

Glencoe Ski Centre: (01855) 851 226; Ski day pass: £27–35 (Jan–Apr), chairlift: £12 (Jul & Aug); www.glencoemountain.co.uk

■ Drive the scenic road that runs parallel to the A82 from Glencoe to the Clachaig Inn.

■ The craft shop in Glencoe has a good menu including delicious desserts.

TOP 10 ⭐ Culzean Castle

Formerly a rather dull fortified tower house, Culzean (pronounced "Cullane") was transformed by the architect Robert Adam into a mansion of sumptuous proportions and elegance. The work began in 1777 and lasted almost 20 years, the Kennedy family sparing little expense in the decoration and craftsmanship of their clifftop home. Culzean – a masterpiece in a land full of magnificent castles – was gifted to the nation and fully restored in the 1970s. Its grounds became Scotland's first public country park in 1969.

4 Oval Staircase

Nothing short of perfection. Ionic and Corinthian capitals swirl above a Georgian-patterned carpet, lit up by an arched skylight **(left)**.

5 Home Farm Visitor Centre

No ordinary farm, but more of a fortified village within the country park; now it is a shop and restaurant.

1 Country Park

Widely regarded as the most magnificent park in Britain **(right)**, this coastal swathe of woodland, ponds, gardens, beaches and clifftop walks retains the Country Park's original character.

2 Lord Cassilis' Rooms

The restored late 18th-century decor includes vivacious Chinese-style wallpaper and a late Chippendale four-poster bed.

6 Round Drawing Room

The most beautiful room in the castle, with its circle of windows overlooking the sea.

3 Armoury

Over 1,000 weapons **(above)** cover the walls in concentric patterns. The fearsome arsenal includes the largest collection of used flintlock pistols in Europe.

ROBERT ADAM

Born in Kinross-shire in 1728, Robert Adam was educated at Edinburgh University. His subsequent tour of Italy determined his Neo-Classical style, and he went on to set up an architectural practice in London, becoming the foremost designer of his day. A passionate worker, his fanaticism for detail was legendary. Adam died in 1792, the year Culzean was completed.

7 Clifftop and Shoreline Trails

The views to the mountains of Arran are glorious from these trails. Two favourite destinations are Swan Pond and Happy Valley. Put on your walking boots and explore the glorious grounds.

Floorplan of Culzean Castle

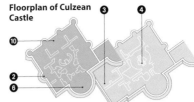

Key to Floorplan

First floor
Ground floor

9 Eisenhower Apartment

The apartment **(below)** on the top floor was a gift to the US president for his support in World War II. It is now a small hotel.

10 Long Drawing Room

Formerly the High Hall of the old tower house, this was the first room that Adam transformed, and it was the first to be restored in the 1970s.

Culzean Castle and gardens

NEED TO KNOW

MAP G3 ▪ Maybole ▪ (01655) 884 455 ▪ www.nts.org.uk

Open Apr–Oct: 10:30am–4:30pm daily; Nov–Mar: shops & restaurant only, 10am–5pm daily; Castle grounds: 9am–sunset daily

Adm (castle & park) adults £13; concessions £9.50; family £46; single-parent family £36; (free for NTS members)

▪ Don't miss the Walled Garden, and its Victorian Vinery, where period species of dessert grapes are grown.

8 Camellia House

This impressive Gothic greenhouse **(below)** is one of more than 40 architectural features found dotted around the grounds. It was designed in 1818 by James Donaldson, a pupil of Robert Adam.

TOP 10 ⭐ The Cairngorms

The highest mountain massif in the British Isles comprises a magnificent range of peaks, wild lochs and ancient forests, as well as bird sanctuaries, nature reserves and sports amenities. It is a region of exceptional scenery and habitats untouched by the road network. Activities take place on its fringe, but the heartland is open only to those who travel by foot or on skis. Its relative isolation makes it appealing for the wildlife that inhabits the region and for the people who thrive on the testing terrain.

1 Aviemore
Traditionally a dormitory town for skiers as well as the jumping-off point for touring the region at any time of the year, Aviemore consists of a concentration of hotels, guesthouses, bars, restaurants and après-ski (or, indeed, après-anything) entertainment.

SPIRIT OF SPEYSIDE WHISKY FESTIVAL

A merry May festival in which you can view illicit stills and the Customs and Excise Contraband Caravan, ride The Whisky Train, dance a Highland Fling and cook your own scones against the clock. The highlight is the opulent whisky dinner set to the sounds of pipe bands.

2 Loch Morlich
Surrounded by the Caledonian pines of Rothiemurchus Forest, Loch Morlich **(above)** is a vast, tranquil lake at the base of the Cairngorms.

3 Loch an Eilean
Loch an Eilean is a hidden gem, 8 km (5 miles) from Aviemore. One of Scotland's best short walks is along this loch, nestling below the mountains. The trees are magnificent, and its crowning glory is an ivy-clad castle on an island.

5 Speyside Wildlife
A short drive from Aviemore, this hidden spot in the Caledonian pine forest is best for watching wildlife including badgers, pine martens **(left)** and more in the evening.

4 River Spey
Scotland's finest salmon river and birthplace of whisky, the Spey **(left)** is a river of dark pools and fast rapids. It winds through a variety of landscapes: moorland, forest, pasture and grain field.

Map of The Cairngorms

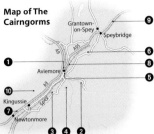

9 Malt Whisky Trail
The process of turning water into the "water of life" is a vital part of Scottish history and culture. Half of the nation's malt whisky distilleries are on Speyside **(above)**, and the signposted "whisky trail" leads the way to seven of them.

10 Cairngorm Reindeer Centre
Britain's only herd of wild reindeer **(right)** was introduced to the Cairngorms in the 1960s. These charming animals, now numbering around 150, roam free.

6 Loch Garten Osprey Centre
Ospreys began breeding here in the late 1950s and each spring they return to Loch Garten from their wintering grounds – the nest site is continually monitored to stop egg collectors.

7 Highland Folk Museum
This open-air museum offers a fantastic cross-section of historical buildings – among them dwellings, a church and a school – that have been moved here from their original location.

8 Strathspey Steam Railway
The train **(below)** chuffs from Aviemore to Broomhill, via Boat Garten through a lovely landscape; for the best views grab a seat on the right-hand side.

NEED TO KNOW

MAP D4–5

Speyside Wildlife: (01479) 812 498; open Easter–Oct nightly; adm adult £25, children 8–14 yrs £10 (not suitable for under 8s); www.speysidewildlife.co.uk

Loch Garten Osprey Centre: (01479) 831 476; open Apr–Aug daily; adm adults £5

Highland Folk Museum: open Apr–Aug: 10:30am–5:30pm daily; Sep & Oct: 11am–4:30pm daily; www.highlandlife.com

Strathspey Steam Railway: (01479) 810 725; open Mar–Oct; return £16.75; www.strathspeyrailway.co.uk

Malt Whisky Trail: www.maltwhisky trail.com

Cairngorm Reindeer Centre: Guided hill visits 11am daily (May–Sep: also 2:30pm); hill trip £18; paddock visits £3.50; www.cairngormreindeer.co.uk

Spirit of Speyside Whisky Festival: open late Apr–early May; free to RSPB members; www.spiritofspeyside.com

The Top 10
of Everything

The Forth Rail Bridge, spanning the
Firth of Forth near Edinburgh

🔟 Moments in History

St Columba, the Irish missionary

1 The Coming of Christianity

The Irish missionary Columba set up a Christian community on the tiny island of Iona in AD 563 and his followers gradually converted the Pictish and Scots kingdoms.

2 Wars of Independence

Robert the Bruce's decisive victory over Edward II at Bannockburn in 1314 ended a 20-year English campaign of conquest. In 1329 a papal bull confirmed Scotland's independence, but wars with England continued on and off for almost 400 years.

3 Battle of Flodden

James IV's invasion of England in 1513 ended at Flodden, where 10,000 Scots (including the King himself) died in battle. With an infant heir, a power struggle and years of instability followed.

1314 Time of Battle of Bannockburn

Robert the Bruce

4 Reformation and Royal Union

From 1559, preacher John Knox led the Protestant Reformation in Scotland, clashing with its Catholic Queen Mary. The Protestant faction ousted Mary in 1568 and enthroned her son James, reinforcing the Reformation but ushering in 150 years of sectarian conflict. When Elizabeth I of England died childless in 1603, her nearest Protestant heir James succeeded to the English throne, uniting the crowns of Scotland and England.

5 Civil Wars and Restoration

Scotland was drawn into England's Civil Wars from 1639, changing sides several times. The country became part of Oliver Cromwell's Commonwealth until the restoration of Charles II in 1660. Under Charles and his successor James II, Scottish religious liberties were stifled and resistance crushed in the "Killing Times" of the 1670s and 80s.

6 A United Kingdom?

The 1707 Act of Union united the two countries and dissolved the Scots parliament, creating the United Kingdom of Great Britain. Risings in favour of the exiled Stuarts followed in 1715 and 1745, ending with the crushing of Charles Edward Stuart's army at Culloden on 16 April 1746 – the last pitched battle on British soil.

7 George IV's Visit to Edinburgh

In 1822, King George IV became the first British monarch to visit Scotland since Charles II in 1651. The event was organized by the Romantic novelist Sir Walter Scott and the king donned Highland dress for the occasion.

8 Transportation and Exile

During the "Radical War" of the 1820s, weavers and other workers fought for the right to vote, but were quickly crushed by government

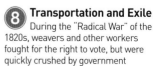

militia. The revolutionaries were either executed or transported to Australia. Also, in an event known as the Clearances, Border lairds and clan chieftains forcibly evicted their tenants in order to make way for sheep pastures, exiling thousands to Canada and other British dominions.

Joseph Black visiting James Watt

9 Industrial Rise and Fall

The Industrial Revolution of the 19th century, driven by James Watt's steam engine, transformed Scotland. Numerous indigent Highlanders and Irish immigrants migrated to Glasgow and Dundee. Mining, iron and steel, shipbuilding and weaving boomed, and Glasgow became known as "the workshop of the Empire". Heavy industry began to decline after World War I and slumped after World War II.

10 Devolution and After

In a 1997 referendum, Scots voted for a devolved Scottish Parliament. Many continued to campaign for full nationhood, but in the 2014 referendum 55 per cent of Scots voted to remain within the UK. Despite this, the SNP remains the single biggest party in the Scottish Parliament, and has pledged a second independence referendum by 2023.

Nicola Sturgeon, leader of the SNP

TOP 10 WRITERS

Kathleen Jamie, Scots Makar in 2021

1 Robert Burns (1759–96)
The famously nationalistic poet achieved worldwide acclaim that titled him "the bard of humanity".

2 Sir Walter Scott (1771–1832)
The first best-selling author, whose novels and poems launched the Romantic tradition.

3 Robert Louis Stevenson (1850–94)
Best known for *Treasure Island*, Stevenson also wrote historical tales including *Kidnapped* and *Catriona*.

4 J M Barrie (1860–1937)
Born in Kirriemuir, this novelist and dramatist established his reputation with the ever-popular *Peter Pan*.

5 Nan Shepherd (1893–1981)
Modernist writer known for her mountain memoir *The Living Mountain*, which was based on her hill walking experiences in the Cairngorms.

6 Alasdair Gray (1934–2019)
Genre-defying Glaswegian artist, dramatist and author who first received literary acclaim for *Lanark* (1981).

7 Val McDermid (1955–)
The queen of the "tartan noir" crime genre and vocalist with rock band *The Fun Lovin' Crime Writers*.

8 Ian Rankin (1960–)
The creator of the hugely successful Inspector Rebus crime series was born in Fife, and now lives in Edinburgh.

9 Kathleen Jamie (1962–)
Appointed Scots Makar (laureate) in 2021, best known as a prolific poet and author of travel and non-fiction books.

10 A L Kennedy (1965–)
Acclaimed Dundee-born author and a winner of numerous literary awards.

🔟 Castles

1 Edinburgh Castle
The greatest castle *(see pp12–13)* in a land that's full of them, not only prized for its crowning position in the capital's heart, but also for its important history and the national treasures it holds.

2 Culzean Castle
Architect Robert Adam's masterful design and exquisite taste reached their apotheosis in this castle *(see pp32–3)*, which ranks as one of Britain's finest mansions. Set in a park that does it ample justice, it commands a dramatic coastal position, looking seaward from the top of an Ayrshire cliff.

3 Caerlaverock Castle
A triangular ruin with immense towers, Caerlaverock *(see p88)* still sits within a filled moat. Its history spans a siege by King Edward I in 1300 and a luxurious upgrading shortly before its fall in 1640. Its yellow sandstone walls glow beautifully pink and orange in the afternoon light.

4 Stirling Castle
Dramatically perched on crags overlooking the plains where some of Scotland's most decisive battles took place, this castle *(see p103)* was one of the nation's greatest strongholds and a key player in her history. The gatehouse, Great Hall and the Renaissance Royal Palace are outstanding.

Check out the castle's programme of special events, from tapestry weaving to sword fights.

5 Glamis Castle
This 17th-century fairy-tale castle *(see p93)* is known for its literary associations: Duncan's Hall provided the setting for the king's murder in Shakespeare's *Macbeth*. It also has a famous secret chamber and was the childhood home of the late Queen Mother. Rooms represent different periods of history and contain fine collections of armour, furnishings and tapestries. The gardens were laid out by 18th-century landscape gardener "Capability" Brown. Besides an Italian garden there are other green spaces, including a walled garden that features fountains, fruits and vegetables. There are nature trails as well.

Glamis Castle

Eilean Donan Castle, on an island in Loch Duich

6 Balmoral

Queen Victoria purchased the Balmoral Estate in 1852 and transformed the existing castle into this imposing mansion set in spectacular grounds. Balmoral *(see p110)* is still the private holiday home of the British royal family, and provides an insight into contemporary stately living.

7 Dunnottar Castle

A glorious ruin *(see p109)* on a clifftop in Aberdeenshire with the sea crashing below, this is one of Scotland's most evocative sights. In the 17th century, the Scottish crown jewels were hidden here, away from Oliver Cromwell's marauding forces. The most scenic way to arrive at the castle is by the coastal footpath from Stonehaven.

8 Cawdor Castle

Whether or not the real Macbeth lived here in the 11th century, Cawdor *(see p111)* is the sort of make-believe castle that has come to life to satisfy all your Shakespearean expectations. The castle is utterly magical, with its original keep (1454), a drawbridge, ancient yew tree and an extensive collection of weapons. The garden and estate are equally enchanting and there's even a maze to get lost in.

9 Eilean Donan Castle

One of Scotland's most photographed castles *(see p118)* because of its incredible setting – huddled on an island off the shores of Loch Duich and connected to the mainland by footbridge. This 13th-century stronghold of the Clan Macrae was left to ruin until its restoration in the 1930s.

10 Blair Castle

Seat of the Duke of Atholl, the only man in Britain still allowed a private army, this stately white castle *(see p91)* is an arresting sight off the A9, the main road north. The oldest part dates from 1269, but after damage during the Jacobite campaigns Blair Castle was completely restyled and all the turrets added.

Drawing room at Blair Castle

📖10 Highland Traditions

Highland dancers in traditional kilts

1 Scottish Dancing

Vital features of any Highland Games are the kilted dancers competing on stage. Among the most common Highland dances are Sword Dances and the Highland Fling. While Highland dancers perform solo, Scottish country dancing is a group affair. These energetic dances, such as Strip the Willow, are often featured at weddings.

2 Kilts and Tartans

Tartan patterned cloth was worn by Celtic peoples as early as the 3rd century AD, but the iconic Scottish kilt and clan tartans are modern creations. Traditional Highland dress was banned after the Jacob rising of 1745. It was revived and reinvented in 1822 with George IV's royal visit, when the king himself wore Highland dress. Since then more than 2,000 designs have been registered, and kilts have become ever more colourful.

3 Common Ridings

Known as the Riding of the Marches, this ritual dates back to the Middle Ages, when young men from the Border towns (such as Hawick)

Bagpipes

would ride out to check the boundaries of the town's common land. Each town has its own ceremony: the oldest is the Selkirk Gathering. Being one of the oldest equestrian events in the world, the Ridings take place early summer and may last several days.

4 Gaelic Language

Once spoken from Argyll and Perthshire to the far northwest and the Hebrides, Gaelic is now spoken by around only 60,000 people, almost all of whom live in the Western Isles. Nonetheless, you'll see road and station signs in Gaelic all over Scotland, even in southern regions where it was never spoken.

5 Bagpipes

No sound is more evocative of Scotland than that of bagpipes. The great Highland pipes, dating back to at least the 14th century, are played by pipe and drum bands, and by individuals playing for competitions or dances. Over the last three decades bagpipes have emerged onto the stage of world music.

6 Curling

This sport (similar to bowls on ice) is one in which the Scots excel at the Winter Olympics. Heavy circular granite stones, with a flat base and a handle on top, are used. The curler slides the stone down the rink towards a bull's-eye, and teammates, polish the path ahead of the stone if more momentum is needed.

7 Shinty

This sport makes football look dull. Similar to anarchic hockey, this fast-moving game is entertaining to watch and usually takes place during winter and spring.

8 The Loonie Dook

Only the brave dare a dip in Scotland's near-freezing North Sea for the annual New Year's Day "Loonie Dook". The first "Loonie Dook" took place in 1986, and has since spawned similar charity events at Portobello (near Edinburgh), St Andrew's and elsewhere.

9 Ceilidhs

Ceilidh ("cay-lee") is Gaelic for "a visit among friends", but has taken on the meaning of "a party". Sometimes it is a hall with a band where everyone dances. At other times it is a communal performance where people sing, dance or play an instrument in turns. They are great fun and even ceilidhs held in the smallest of village halls host world-class local or touring performers.

10 Highland Games

This summer spectacle is packed with bagpipes, dancers and athletes, and forms an essential part of any visit. Most popular are the kilted strongmen in the "heavy events", which include hurling monstrous hammers as well as tossing a tree trunk.

The caber toss, Highland Games

🔟 Lochs

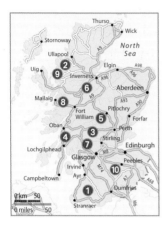

1 Loch Trool
MAP H4

An enchanting loch within a forest, in a much overlooked corner of Scotland, characterized by its stunning wilderness. The loch is bordered by walks, which form part of the long-distance Southern Upland Way *(see p52)*. At the eastern end there's a memorial to King Robert the Bruce, King of Scots from 1306 until his death in 1329.

2 Loch Maree
MAP C3

You'll pass this loch if you visit Inverewe Gardens *(see p49)*. Wonderfully situated among imposing mountains, Loch Maree is a revered fishing location next to a nature reserve. Red deer have been known to swim out to the group of wooded islands in the centre and make temporary homes there.

Picturesque Loch Maree

3 Loch Katrine
MAP F4

Famous as the inspiration for Sir Walter Scott's poem *Lady of the Lake*, this loch is the pearl of the area known as the Trossachs. Now incorporated into the National Park with Loch Lomond *(see p103)*, it is sheer tranquillity compared with the other's bustle. A boat tour here is highly recommended – the SS *Sir Walter Scott* (naturally) has been doing the job for over a century.

4 Loch Awe
MAP F3

A long sliver of a loch, twisting through forested hills and dotted with islets. The remarkable St Conan's Kirk *(see p106)* stands near the north end of the loch, as do the magnificent ruins of the 13th-century Kilchurn Castle. Take the southern road for the best scenery, and don't be in a hurry.

Ruins of Kilchurn Castle at Loch Awe

5 Loch Tummel
MAP E4

This small loch, with its shimmering brilliance, was a favourite of Queen Victoria, and you can stand at her

Lush forest around Loch Tummel

preferred spot on the north side at Queen's View. The vista to the distant peak of Schiehallion *(see p47)* is splendid, complemented in autumn by sweeps of colourful forest. Take the southern road to find the best picnic spots by the loch, and don't miss the river gorge walks at nearby Killiecrankie *(see p94)*.

⑥ Loch Ness
MAP D4

Probably Scotland's most charismatic loch *(see pp28–9)*, this deep body of water is a major draw for its scenic splendour of the Great Glen, Urquhart Castle and the as-yet-unexplained sightings of monster Nessie.

⑦ Loch Lomond

The largest surface of fresh water in Scotland, Loch Lomond's *(see p103)* beauty is celebrated in literature, song and legend. Forming part of Scotland's first National Park, in conjunction with the Trossachs, the loch is revered for its islands, lofty hills and shoreside leisure facilities.

⑧ Loch Morar

The rival to Loch Ness, Loch Morar *(see p120)* is Scotland's deepest loch at over 300 m (1,000 ft), and has long had its own legend of a monster – Morag (apparently identical to Nessie). Morar is easy to get to but seldom visited because its shores are largely inaccessible to cars, which makes it all the more delightful for walking *(see p58)*. Nearby are spectacular beaches – the White Sands of Morar.

⑨ Loch Torridon
MAP D3

A magnificent sea loch that is reminiscent of a Norwegian fjord. The wall of red sandstone mountains to its north attracts hill walkers, and from the summits you can see all the way from Cape Wrath *(see p129)* to Ardnamurchan *(see p118)*. A lovely one-way walk takes you from Diabeg to Inveralligin, with a series of refreshing lochans (small lochs) for swimming if the weather's hot.

⑩ Loch Skeen
MAP G5

The hidden treasure at the end of an utterly magical walk, Loch Skeen is a tiny loch high up in moorland hills. The walk to it climbs steeply alongside the spectacular Grey Mare's Tail waterfall (note that it's dangerous to leave the path en route). The visitor centre, situated near the falls, has a CCTV on a peregrine falcon nest.

🔟 Munros

① Ben Nevis

Britain's highest mountain (see p117) at 1,345 m (4,413 ft). A long, winding path takes you up to the top. The summit is seldom clear of cloud, but if you strike it lucky you'll enjoy unsurpassed views. In poor visibility take great care on the summit ridge as it's easy to lose the path, which borders a precipice.

Climbing Ben Nevis

② Ben Cruachan
MAP E3

A grouping of seven peaks overlooking lochs Awe (see p44) and Etive. The highest is 1,126 m (3,694 ft) and as this summit is considerably taller than any other mountain in the area, Ben Cruachan enjoys some of the most extensive views in the country. The name "Cruachan" comes from the war cry of the Campbell clan (see p43).

③ Ben Macdui
MAP D5

Britain's second-highest mountain, at 1,309 m (4,295 ft), is best climbed from the Cairngorm ski car park. Reached by a high-altitude plateau covered in Arctic flora, it overlooks the magnificent Lairig Ghru, a deep rift dividing the Cairngorm range.

Soaring Ben Macdui

WHAT IS A MUNRO?

Any Scottish summit over 3,000 ft (approx. 900 m) is called a "Munro" after Sir Hugh Munro, who published a list of them in 1891. There are 282 Munros, and "Munro-bagging" is a popular pastime. Most can be walked safely without climbing skills, but it is vital to plan well and be properly equipped and competent in map-reading. Conditions can deteriorate rapidly at any time of year.

④ Ben Vorlich
MAP F4

A great one to start with as there's nothing complicated about this hill, which overlooks Loch Earn, always bustling with boat activity. Take the southern road and start from Ardvorlich. At the top, at 985 m (3,232 ft), the views to the Breadalbane mountains are glorious. After drinking it in and taking some panoramic snaps, it doesn't take long to get down for tea in St Fillans.

⑤ Ben Lomond
MAP F4

Rising proudly from the wooded banks of its namesake loch, Ben Lomond's tall mass dominates the panorama. One of the smallest Munros at 973 m (3,192 ft), it has a well-used track, which is steep in places. There are tremendous views over the Loch Lomond and Trossachs National Park (see p103). It is best to start at Rowardennan, where there's a hotel and hostel.

⑥ Ben Hope
MAP B4

The most northerly Munro, with its neighbour, Foinaven. Rising starkly from the woods and moorland around Loch Hope, 927-m (3,040-ft) Ben Hope has clear views to the Orkneys. The only difficulty in bagging this peak is the scree and rocky terrain, but this is a prestigious mountain to have underfoot.

The Five Sisters, reflected in the waters of Loch Duich

7 The Five Sisters
MAP D3

A superb range of mountains with five prominent peaks towering above Glen Shiel in the West Highlands. Start at the highest part of the main road (A87) to save yourself an hour's climbing. Once you're on the summit ridge it's a long series of undulations, but you feel on top of the world and can see the Cuillins on Skye (see pp26–7).

8 Buchaille Etive Mor
MAP E3

The 1,021-m- (3,350-ft-) tall "Great Shepherd of Etive" stands as guardian to the eastern entrance to Glencoe (see pp30–31). As an introduction to a place of legendary beauty, this wild mountain could not be improved. Approached from the southwest it can be climbed easily, but its magnificent crags demand respect.

9 Schiehallion
MAP E4

A much-loved mountain between lochs Tay and Rannoch, Schiehallion is most easily climbed from the pretty road connecting Aberfeldy with Tummel Bridge. An easy and rewarding Munro with which to launch your bagging campaign.

10 Liathach
MAP D3

You could pick any of the famous Torridon mountains (see p116) and guarantee not to be disappointed, but this is a particular beauty. A massive mound of red sandstone topped with white quartzite, Liathach has distinctive parallel bands of escarpments. At 1,055 m (3,461 ft), this is a relatively difficult and strenuous mountain to climb, but worth every bit of effort.

Liathach from Loch na Frianach

🔟 Gardens

Rock garden at the Royal Botanic Garden, Edinburgh

① Royal Botanic Garden

Edinburgh's prize garden (see p76), founded in 1670 and moved to its current site in 1820, features huge trees, rock terraces and borders bursting with colour. The glasshouses are of particular interest, containing everything from hothouse palm trees and gigantic lilies to dwarf cactuses and orchids. Watch out for special events, such as music, theatre and exhibitions of contemporary art.

② Dawyck Botanic Garden

MAP G5 ▪ Stobo, nr Peebles ▪ (01721) 760254 ▪ Open Apr–Sep: 10am–6pm daily (Mar & Oct: to 5pm; Feb & Nov: to 4pm) ▪ Adm

An outpost of Edinburgh's Royal Botanic Garden, where trees are the speciality. They began planting them here 300 years ago. With its enormous diversity and fine specimens, the garden is ideal for woodland walks. The visitor centre has a café, a shop and exhibitions.

③ Kailzie Gardens

MAP G5 ▪ Kailzie, nr Peebles ▪ (01721) 720007 ▪ Open Apr–Oct: 10am–5pm daily; Nov–Mar: daylight hours daily ▪ Adm ▪ www.kailzie gardens.com

This formal walled garden is an outstanding example of what was once more common on family estates. Marvellous roses fill the air with fragrance, and there's a pond stocked with trout for fishing.

④ Logan Botanic Garden

MAP H3 ▪ Port Logan, south of Stranraer ▪ (01776) 860231 ▪ Open Mar–Oct: 10am–5pm daily (Nov: to 4pm; Feb: to 4pm Sun only) ▪ Adm ▪ www.rbge.org.uk

The Logan has the largest number of sub-tropical species growing outdoors in Scotland. The palm trees and gunnera have grown to almost jungle proportions. Apart from the climate, there's a South Pacific feel to the place. It's usually much quieter than other gardens.

5 Botanic Gardens, Glasgow

Positively bulging with greenery and colour, Glasgow's Botanic Gardens (see p99) are a favourite with locals and visitors alike. The magnificent gardens date from 1817, and are particularly noted for their glasshouses. Foremost among these is the curved iron framework of the restored Kibble Palace. An oasis of palm trees, ferns, orchids, begonias and many tropical species is found inside. Art exhibitions, theatre, festivals and plant shows also take place here.

6 Crarae Gardens

Created in 1912 by Lady Grace Campbell, this Himalayan-style woodland garden (see p104) has one of the country's most diverse collections of rhododendrons. Many of the seeds were gathered on private expeditions around the world and some species are now rare. In May the garden bursts into a mass of blooms. It is also home to the National Collection of southern beech trees. There is a waterfall, a gorge and several walking trails.

7 Arduaine Gardens

Overlooking the sea, this garden (see p104) was established in 1898. It is another famous rhododendron collection, but includes blue Tibetan poppies, giant Himalayan lilies, lush magnolias, camellias, tree ferns, water lilies and Chatham Island forget-me-nots. Having fallen into disrepair, Arduaine was lovingly restored by two brothers. See wildlife such as red squirrels in the woods, or spot seals and porpoises at the sea shore.

Rhododendrons, Arduaine Gardens

Plants at The Hydroponicum

8 The Hydroponicum

A totally revolutionary place, the "garden of the future" (see p120) has no soil but uses a clever water irrigation system to carry nutrients to the plants. Take a tour of the growing houses where they cultivate everything from tropical flowers to bananas. You can buy your own growing kits and fresh seasonal produce.

9 Inverewe Gardens

A west coast phenomenon, these much-vaunted gardens (see p119) are worth travelling a long way to see. The gardens were nurtured into astonishing fertility in 1862 by Scottish aristocrat Osgood Mackenzie on his 8.5-sq-km (3-sq-mile) estate, and they became his life's work. Plants, shrubs and trees from all over the world form one of the finest botanical collections in the country, all in a stunning location on Loch Ewe.

10 Pitmedden Garden

Originally laid out in a Classical French style in 1675 and destroyed by a fire in 1818, Pitmedden (see p109) was meticulously recreated in the 1950s. The effect is stunning. Within a vast walled area are four elaborate floral parterres, three of which have heraldic designs.

⏹ Walking Routes

Breathtaking sights from Conic Hill, West Highland Way

① West Highland Way
MAP E3–F4 ▪ 154 km (96 miles) ▪ 7–10 days ▪ www.westhighland way.org

The first long-distance route, and still the most popular. Connecting Fort William and Glasgow, it winds past the Nevis and Glencoe ranges, crosses Rannoch Moor and skirts around every other mountain it can find. Stunning scenery, but rather close to the main road in parts.

② Southern Upland Way
MAP H3–F6 ▪ 344 km (214 miles) ▪ 15–20 days ▪ www. dgtrails.org/southern-upland-way

Britain's first official coast-to-coast route is a wonderful mix of mountain, moor, forest, loch and pasture. It crosses the country from Portpatrick in the west to Cockburnspath in the east – the preferred direction if you want the wind at your back.

③ Great Glen Way
MAP D4–E3 ▪ 127 km (79 miles) ▪ 4–7 days ▪ www. highland.gov.uk/greatglenway

This popular long-distance route probably packs in more dramatic scenery per mile than any other.

The walk connects Fort William with Inverness. The southern half offers easier gradients along the banks of lochs Lochy and Oich. After Fort Augustus it climbs high above Loch Ness – if that doesn't take your breath, the views will.

④ Speyside Way
MAP D4–C5 ▪ 105 km (66 miles) ▪ 4–6 days ▪ www.speysideway.org

Bordering one of Scotland's most picturesque rivers, this path takes you from the Cairngorms to Moray's coast (with spurs to Dufftown and Tomintoul). It is a walk full of interest, with distilleries galore, bridges, stately homes and a rich abundance of wildlife.

⑤ Borders Abbeys Way
MAP G5–6 ▪ 105 km (65 miles) ▪ 4–5 days ▪ www.scotborders.gov. uk/bordersabbeysway

Borders Abbeys Way is a circular route that combines historical interest with the irresistible appeal of the gentle Borders landscape, with its rounded hills, rivers and forests. The track connects the four magnificent abbeys of Kelso, Melrose, Dryburgh and Jedburgh.

Previous pages Steam train crossing the Glenfinnan Viaduct on the West Highland Line

6 Cateran Trail
MAP E5 ■ 103 km (64 miles)
■ **5 days** ■ www.pkct.org/cateran-trail

The Caterans, brigands and rustlers roamed this area in the Middle Ages. Starting in Blairgowrie's soft-fruit hills, this circular route wends to the wild mountains of Glenshee, returning via beautiful Glenisla, offering some of the best of Perthshire. This is a quieter trail than most.

7 Fife Coastal Path
MAP F5 ■ 188 km (117 miles)
■ **6–9 days** ■ www.fifecoastand
countrysidetrust.co.uk/walks/fife-
coastal-path

This walk connects the famous Forth and Tay bridges. It runs from North Queensferry, near Deep Sea World, to the small fishing villages of the East Neuk such as Elie and Anstruther, which huddle beside rugged cliffs. The route then heads north, through the historic town and golfing capital of St Andrews.

Newark Castle, Fife Coastal Path

8 St Cuthbert's Way
MAP G5–6 ■ 100 km (62 miles)
■ **4 days** ■ www.stcuthbertsway.info

This is the only cross-border route in Scotland. It starts in the abbey town of Melrose and ends on the amazing island of Lindisfarne (England). It is not too strenuous a walk and a lovely mix of pasture, woodland, moor and coastal scenery. Be sure to check the tides for the last mile.

9 Loch Lomond and Cowal Way
MAP F3 ■ 92 km (57 miles)
■ **7 days** ■ www.lochlomondand
cowalway.org

If you like things a little wilder, try this one. The route is fully waymarked, and passes through some of Scotland's most varied landscapes– so take a good map. Start on the coast west of Glasgow at Portavadie and cross the hills of the Cowal peninsula to Inveruglas on the shores of Loch Lomond.

10 John Muir Way
MAP F4–6 ■ 215 km
(134 miles) ■ 7–10 days
■ www.johnmuirway.org

This route runs coast to coast, from Helensburgh in the west to Dunbar in the east. Named for John Muir, father of America's National Parks, who was born in Dunbar.

John Muir Way

TOP 10 Journeys

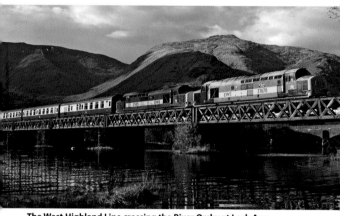

The West Highland Line crossing the River Orchy at Loch Awe

1 West Highland Line
MAP D2–F4 ■ ScotRail: www.
scotrail.co.uk ■ Jacobite Steam Train:
www.westcoastrailways.co.uk

The West Highland Line runs from
Glasgow to Mallaig. The journey takes
around 5 hours and 30 minutes, and
the train stops frequently, giving the
chance to relax and enjoy the sights
of Scotland's west coast. Look out for
the Glenfinnan Viaduct, which featured
in the *Harry Potter* films, as well as
views of Ben Nevis and Loch Eilt. If you
want to travel in style take the Jacobite
Steam Train which runs in summer.

2 Take Flight
Loch
Lomond Sea-
planes: (01436)
675 030; www.
lochlomond-
seaplanes.com
■ Loganair: www.
loganair.co.uk

Seaplane, Loch Lomond

Soar over Loch
Lomond or the Isle
of Skye with Loch Lomond Seaplanes.
The seaplane offers spectacular
views of Scotland's lochs and moun-
tains. Tours should be booked ahead.
Another exhilarating flight is from
Glasgow to Barra with Loganair.

The island's runway is on a beach
and disappears under the waves
when the tide comes in.

3 Borders Railway
MAP F5–G5 ■ www.borders
railway.co.uk

Opened in 2015 and stretching 56 km
(35 miles) between Edinburgh and
Tweedbank, the Borders Railway is
the longest railway line to be built
in Britain for 100 years. Tweedbank
station is a short walk from Abbotsford
House, home of Sir Walter Scott.

4 The Road to the Isles
MAP D2–E3

The A830 from Fort
William to Mallaig is
known as the 'Road
to the Isles'. This is
Bonnie Prince
Charlie country
and is crammed
with Jacobite his-
tory. Driving it gives you
the freedom to stop and explore sights,
such as Glenfinnan, where Charles
Edward Stuart placed his standard in
1745 and rallied the clans in his attempt
to regain the crown; and Loch nan
Uamh, from where he fled to France
after being defeated at Culloden.

⑤ Steam Back in Time
MAP F4 ■ www.waverley
excursions.co.uk

A trip "doon the watter" on the PS *Waverley*, the world's last seagoing paddle steamer, is a classic Scottish journey that all ages can enjoy. Launched in 1946 and originally fuelled by coal, the ship was saved from the breaker's yard in the 1970s and is now owned by a charity. Take a summer day trip from Glasgow to destinations such as Dunoon, Rothesay and Arran. Special excursions run too.

⑥ Climb a Mountain
www.cairngormmountain.co.uk

From the gentler slopes of the Eildon Hills in the Borders, to the mighty peak of Ben Nevis, Scotland's hills and mountains are wild, beautiful, challenging and irresistible. If you are not an experienced walker, or don't fancy going alone, rangers offer weekly guided walks around the Northern Corries of the Cairngorms.

⑦ Pedal a Trail
7 Stanes Centres:
www.forestryandland.gov.scot

Whether you're a novice or an experienced biker, you're sure to find a trail to suit you in Scotland. There are demanding routes such as the Sligachan on Skye, a single-track circuit almost 45 km (28 miles) long. The 7 Stanes Centres, in Dumfries and Galloway and the Borders, offer trails to suit all abilities. They have centres at Dalbeattie, Glentrool, Ae, Kirroughtree, Mabie, Glentress and Innerleithen and Newcastleton.

Bike trail

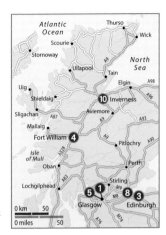

⑧ Bridge the Forth
MAP F5

When it opened in 1890, the Forth Bridge was the world's longest single-span cantilevered bridge, and it's still an iconic structure. Appreciate this Victorian marvel by taking the train across it – travelling from Edinburgh or South Queensferry into Fife.

⑨ Ferry Crossing
Calmac: www.calmac.co.uk
■ Skye Ferry: operates Easter–Oct:
10am–6pm (Jun–Aug: to 7pm);
www.skyeferry.co.uk

A ferry-trip to a Scottish island is a wonderfully romantic experience. The main operators, Calmac, run services to islands – Arran, Skye and the Inner and Outer Hebrides. Ferries also run between Gourock and Dunoon and connect with trains from Glasgow Central. Scotland's last manually operated turntable ferry, the Skye Ferry, sails between Glenelg on the mainland and Kylerhea on Skye.

⑩ North Coast 500
MAP B5–D4 ■ www.north
coast500.com

The North Coast 500 is an 800-km (500-mile) circuit. From Inverness, the route goes west to Applecross then up the coast and along the tip of Scotland to John O'Groats, from where it heads back down to Inverness.

Golf Courses

1 St Andrews
Every golfer dreams of playing here *(see p92)*. There are seven courses, including the famous Old Course. Book months in advance or take your chance in the lottery for unreserved places held the day before. Fit in a visit to the Golf Museum too, home to 17,000 objects showing the history of golf from the Middle Ages to the present. The restaurant at the Old Course Hotel *(see p95)* is excellent.

Playing at the Old Course, St Andrews

2 Turnberry
MAP G3 ■ (01655) 331 000
■ www.turnberry.co.uk
Purchased by Donald Trump in 2014 and situated on the Ayrshire coast, the Ailsa Course has tested all the world's great players. A new 18-hole course, King Robert the Bruce, opened in 2017. For expert tuition and a review of your game, contact the Golf Academy, a multi-million-pound addition to the hotel.

3 Carnoustie Championship Course
MAP E5 ■ (01241) 802 270
■ www.carnoustiegolflinks.co.uk
A delightful course, the superb links and great character of which have earned it a world-class reputation. You'll need to present your handicap certificate to play here and reserve your tee time in advance, but there are two other good links if you don't get on the main one. Saturdays can be busy throughout the year.

4 Gullane
MAP F5 ■ (01620) 842 255
■ www.gullanegolfclub.co.uk
Almost every blade of grass in this corner of East Lothian is dedicated to golf. Muirfield is the elite course but a private club. Gullane No.1 is open to anyone (handicap certificate required), while Nos. 2 and 3 have no restrictions. If Gullane is crowded, drive a short way to North Berwick, Haddington or Aberlady, and seven more top courses.

5 Muirfield
MAP F5 ■ Gullane ■ (01620) 842 123 ■ www.muirfield.org.uk
This 18-hole championship course dates back to 1891, when it was first laid out by Tom Morris. Situated in lush East Lothian, by the pretty village of Gullane, it is home to the Honourable Company of Edinburgh Golfers. Visitors' days are Tuesday and Thursday. Availability of tee times can be checked in advance.

The grand Turnberry Hotel

Fairway bunkers on Gleneagles golf course

6 Gleneagles
MAP F4 ▪ (01764) 662 231
▪ www.gleneagles.com

Another legendary group of courses, in beautiful moorland attached to a luxurious hotel. There are three championship courses, including the PGA Centenary that was designed by Jack Nicklaus. There is also the PGA National Academy, a nine-hole course, which is ideal for beginners. There is a delectable restaurant here (see p95).

7 Troon
MAP G4 ▪ Old Course & Portland: (01292) 311 555; www.royaltroon.co.uk ▪ Darley, Fullarton, Lochgreen, Kilmarnock: (01292) 616 255; www.golfsouthayrshire.com/courses

Among the eight courses here there's one for everyone, from Fullarton's fun course for beginners to the classics such as Darley and Portland. But the best is the Old Course, a vintage Open venue. You need to apply well in advance.

8 Old Prestwick
MAP G4 ▪ (01292) 477 404
▪ www.prestwickgc.co.uk

New courses come and steal the limelight but Old Prestwick glows as an enduring favourite. In 1860 it was the first venue to hold the British Open Championship. It remains a challenging course and one of Scotland's most venerated. Very busy, especially at weekends.

9 Royal Dornoch
MAP C4 ▪ (01862) 810 219
▪ www.royaldornoch.com

The championship course has 18 pristine holes. It was laid out by Tom Morris in 1877 and follows the natural contours of the dunes around Dornoch Bay. A wonderful setting and less pressurized than other quality links.

10 Nairn
MAP D4 ▪ Nairn: (01667) 453 208; www.nairngolfclub.co.uk ▪ Nairn Dunbar: (01667) 452 741; www.nairndunbar.com

There are two championship courses here. The Nairn hosts major tournaments but also has a nine-hole course, the Cameron, for holiday golfers. Nairn Dunbar is the other top-notch course.

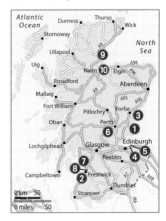

🔟 Off the Beaten Track

Boats moored by the entrance to Morar River

1 Walk from Loch Morar to Tarbet

MAP E3 ■ 20 km (12 miles); approx 6 hours ■ Book the ferry in advance: (01687) 462 233; www.westernisles cruises.co.uk

A combined walk and boat trip through sublime scenery. From Morar's silver sands, follow Britain's shortest river (half a mile) to the loch. Tarred at first, the way turns into an undulating track, which wends to its destination at the lovely bay of Tarbet. Arrive by 3:30pm to catch the ferry back to Mallaig.

2 Old Forge Music Venue

MAP D3 ■ Inverie ■ (01687) 462 267; www.theoldforge.co.uk

Threatened with closure, this much-loved pub – claimed to be the most remote in Britain and accessible only on foot or by boat – was saved by a community buyout in March 2022. The bar has a great range of cask ales, craft beers and malt whiskeys. Live music performances take place fortnightly on Sundays.

3 Sunset from Craig Mountain Bothy

MAP C3 ■ Mountain Bothies Association: www.mountainbothies. org.uk

A simple, isolated cottage with five-star views over the sea to Skye and the Western Isles – sunsets are utterly breathtaking. Only accessible by foot, Craig is 5 km (3 miles) from Little Diabeg or 9 km (5 miles) from Red Point – and a lovely walk it is, too. You'll need to bring all provisions and a sleeping bag, and bear in mind there's no phone on site.

4 Falls of Foyers

MAP D4

The more rain, the merrier for this one, so leave your visit until after a wet day. The upper falls are impressive; the lower falls even more so, plunging a spectacular 62 m (200 ft). The yellow-white torrent gushes into a black bowl, hollowed deep in the forest near Loch Ness, and the almighty roar of the rushing water is as awe-inspiring as the magnificent sight itself.

Falls of Foyers on the River Foyers

5 Elie Chain Walk
MAP F5

As exciting as it is short, this 2.5-km (1.5-mile) cliff walk involves steep carved steps and chains bolted into rock to allow high-tide access between the coves. The best route is to walk west along the cliffs from the small town of Elie, descend to sea level at the tip of the headland, and then return along the chain walk. The chains are inaccessible for 2 hours at high tide, and are unnecessary at low tide.

6 Knoydart
MAP D3 ▪ www.knoydart.org
▪ www.visitknoydart.co.uk

The most remote part of mainland Britain, this peninsula of rugged hills and glens lies in a time warp that's inaccessible by car. However, regular ferries from Mallaig provide access to the village of Inverie and outdoor activities including guided walks and mountain biking. Knoydart is a favourite destination for landscape photographers, which says much about its beauty.

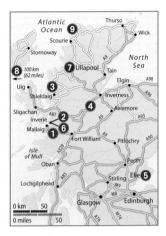

Loch Hourn, Knoydart

7 Drive from Ullapool to Kylesku
MAP C3–B3

Scotland's most beautiful road. Drive it in spring when it's almost consumed by yellow-flowering whins, or in winter when surf erupts against the shore, or on a blue summer evening when Assynt's mountains assume the shape of absurd scribbles. But do drive it: take the A835 north from Ullapool, go west at Drumrunie, follow signs to Lochinver, then the B869 to Kylesku.

8 St Kilda
www.nts.org.uk

Scotland's first World Heritage Site, this archipelago of monumental cliffs was, until 1930, inhabited by a highly individual community who lived off the islands' millions of seabirds. Such is St Kilda's isolation that it has its own subspecies of mouse, wren and sheep. Hard to get to, but if you can it'll touch your soul.

9 Sandwood Bay
MAP B3 ▪ Nr Kinlochbervie

Perhaps it's the colourful strata patterning the rocks (Lewisian gneiss, among the world's oldest) or the quality of the sand. Perhaps it's the huge stack that stands sentinel at one end like some antediluvian shepherd. Or the Atlantic waves that charge in with billowing crests. Or is it the fact that so often you can have this expanse of beach to yourself?

10 Regional Feis
Feb–Oct ▪ Feisean nan Gaidheal: (01478) 613 355
▪ www.feisean.org

A feis ("faysh") is a festival of Gaelic arts combined with workshops. Lasting several days, most take place in the Highlands and Islands, always with terrific performances and energetic dances.

 Children's Attractions

Go Ape treetop trail

1 Go Ape
www.goape.co.uk
Enjoy zip-wiring and treetop thrills in Glentress Forest, near Peebles; Crathes Castle *(see p112)*, near Aberdeen and Queen Elizabeth Forest Park, near Loch Lomond – the last includes a 400-m (1,300-ft) zip wire over a 27-m- (90-ft-) high waterfall.

2 Museum of Childhood
A feast of nostalgia, with toys from the 18th to 21st centuries, this place *(see p15)* is a real family attraction. It features everything – from teddy bears to Teletubbies, Meccano sets to snakes and ladders, comics to satchels and slates. Highlights include a wooden doll dating to around 1740, a tiny Steiff teddy bear which travelled out of Vienna in 1939 on the last Kindertransport train and a dolls house with electric lighting.

3 Our Dynamic Earth
Housed in a spiked tent, this electrifying exhibition *(see p76)* is a mix of education and entertainment. You travel through all sorts of environments, from volcanic eruptions to the Ice Ages. Stand on shaking floors, get caught in a tropical downpour, fly over prehistoric Scottish glaciers and come face-to-face with extinct dinosaurs. The exhibition also goes further, looking at our future and pondering the realities of climate change.

4 M&D's Scotland's Theme Park
MAP F4 ■ Motherwell ■ (01698) 333 777 ■ Open mid-Mar–mid-Oct: times vary, check website ■ Adm ■ www.scotlandsthemepark.com
Huge fairground fun centre with everything that gravitational and centrifugal forces can do to you. Big wheel, free-fall machine, flying carpet, kamikaze whirligigs and the giant "500 tons of twisted fun" roller-coaster. For the younger children there are gentler water chutes and merry-go-rounds. There's also Amazonia, an indoor tropical rainforest.

5 Kelburn Country Centre
MAP F3 ■ Nr Largs ■ (01475) 568 685 ■ Adventure Park & Secret Forest: open Apr–Oct: 10am–6pm daily ■ Grounds: open all year ■ Adm ■ www.kelburnestate.com
The family estate of the Earls of Glasgow doubles as an adventure park. There's an indoor play barn and adventure play areas, as well as a 12th-century castle decorated with graffiti. The Secret Forest, a highlight, is a winding trail dotted with colourful attractions, including a fairy-tale Gingerbread House.

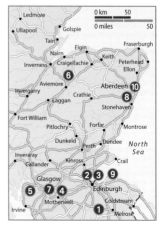

Runaway Timber Train ride at Landmark Forest Adventure Park

6 Landmark Forest Adventure Park

MAP D4 ■ Carrbridge, nr Aviemore ■ (0800) 731 3446 ■ Open Apr–Oct: 10am–6pm daily (mid-Jul–mid-Aug: to 7pm; closing times vary, check website) ■ Adm ■ www.landmark park.co.uk

A play and adventure centre with treetop trails, climbing walls, a Lost Labyrinth maze and a handful of rides. The top attraction is the Dinosaur Kingdom which features over 20 life-size animated models.

7 Glasgow Science Centre

MAP Y3 ■ 50 Pacific Quay, Glasgow ■ (0141) 420 5000 ■ Open Apr–Oct: 10am–5pm (Nov–Mar: to 3pm Wed–Fri, 5pm Sat & Sun) ■ Adm ■ www.glasgowsciencecentre.org

Housed in a landmark building, three floors of hands-on experiments puzzle and delight with miraculous science. There's an IMAX screen and the world's first revolving tower.

8 The Den & The Glen

MAP D6 ■ Maryculter, nr Aberdeen ■ (01224) 732 941 ■ Open 9:30am–5:30pm daily (last entry 4pm) ■ Adm ■ www.denandtheglen.co.uk

A family theme park with giant-sized models of nursery rhyme and story-book characters for kids to explore

and enter make-believe worlds. Humpty Dumpty, Pooh and Postman Pat are among those present and there's a good indoor play area too known as the Den.

9 Scottish Seabird Centre

Zoom in on the wildlife of the Firth of Forth islands (the Bass Rock, Craigleith, Fidra and the Isle of May) using the interactive live cameras without disturbing them here *(see p88)*. See gannets, kittiwakes, razorbills, guillemots, cormorants, puffins and, between October and December, grey seals with their pups. There have been sightings of bottle-nose dolphins, porpoises and even whales. The centre also offers boat trips to the Bass Rock or Isle of May.

Gannet, Bass Rock

10 Beach Leisure Centre

MAP D6 ■ Beach Promenade, Aberdeen ■ (01224) 507 739 ■ Open daily (flume times vary) ■ Adm

Aberdeen has several swimming pools, but this is the one for flumes. There's a mini-flume for tots, but older children will be after the hairiest and scariest: the Pipeline, Wipeout and Tube; the last of these you ride on a tyre. There's also a fun-filled wave machine, as well as a fountain and rapids.

🔟 Whisky Distilleries

Whisky barrels at Springbank

① Springbank
MAP G2 ■ Campbeltown
■ (01586) 552 009 ■ Check for tour
timings ■ Adm ■ www.springbank.scot

Campbeltown was once a whisky
smuggling centre, and the Springbank
distillery, dating back to 1828, was
built on the site of an illicit still. This
independent, family-owned business
produces three distinctive malts –
Springbank, Longrow and Hazelburn –
offering a choice of tours and tastings.

② Glenlivet
MAP D5 ■ Ballindalloch
■ (01340) 821 720 ■ Open Mar–early
Nov: 9am–6pm daily (last entry
4:30pm) ■ www.theglenlivet.com

One of the first distilleries to be
legalized in 1824, the Glenlivet has
been at the forefront of the industry
ever since. A comprehensive tour
includes the musty warehouse where
the whisky ages for 12 to 18 years.

③ Laphroaig
MAP G2 ■ Nr Port Ellen,
Islay ■ (01496) 302 418 ■ Check
for tour timings ■ Adm
■ www.laphroaig.com

With their heavy smoked-peat
flavour, the Islay malts really are in
a class of their own. Even if you think
you won't like them, try them! This
malt is pronounced "la-froyg", but
in truth your pronunciation doesn't
matter – the taste is famous enough
for instant recognition. A delightfully
informal and intimate tour with
plenty of wit and grist at a fine
sea-edge location.

④ Talisker
MAP D2 ■ (01478) 614 308
■ Adm ■ www.malts.com

Skye's original distillery has been
producing a highly respected malt
since 1830. Lively, informative tours
last 40 minutes. Tours are organized
all through the year but are less
frequent in winter. Make sure to
book ahead in summer.

⑤ Lagavulin
MAP G2 ■ Port Ellen, Islay
■ (01496) 302 749 ■ Check for tour
timings ■ Adm ■ www.malts.com

Like its rival Laphroaig, this is a
distinctive malt. Lagavulin whisky is
made in a traditional distillery with
unusual pear-shaped stills. The tour
is highly personal
and free of mass-
market hustle.

**Lagavulin
distillery**

LAGAVULIN

greats), but the best tour. Maybe because they're so remote, they try harder. Prepare to be taken through deep piles of malt drying in a delicious reek of peat.

9 Cardhu
MAP D5 ■ Knockando
■ (01479) 874 635 ■ Check for tour timings ■ Adm ■ www.malts.com

The only distillery to have been pioneered by a woman and, aside from producing a distinguished single malt, it provides the heart of the Johnnie Walker blend. This is one of the smaller distilleries that has a range of tours, all offering a taste of Cardhu.

10 Macallan
MAP D5 ■ Craigellachie
■ (01340) 318 000 ■ Open Easter–Sep: 9:30am–6pm Mon–Sat (Oct–Easter: to 5pm Mon–Fri) ■ Adm
■ www.themacallan.com

Macallan is another of the famous Speyside brands, and the distillery features one of the most modern visitor centres in the valley. Aside from a guided tour, you explore whisky-making using the latest interactive technology. You can become a connoisseur by prearranging an individually tutored nosing and tasting tour.

Copper sills, Edradour distillery

6 Edradour
MAP E5 ■ Nr Pitlochry
■ (01796) 472 095 ■ Tours mid-Apr–mid-Oct: Mon–Fri ■ Adm ■ www.edradour.com

Established in 1825, Edradour claims to be Scotland's smallest distillery and its cluster of buildings has remained virtually unchanged since the 1860s. To witness the process here is all the more delightful for its being in miniature. Only 12 casks a week are produced, making the screigh (as they say) "a rare treat for a few".

7 Glenfarclas
MAP D5 ■ Ballindalloch
■ (01807) 500 345 ■ Open Oct–Mar & Apr–Sep: Mon–Fri; Jul–Sep: also Sat; check for tour timings ■ Adm ■ www.glenfarclas.com

One of the few independent companies and justly proud of it. Established in 1836, this distillery is still owned and managed by the fifth generation of the Grant family. Tour the gleaming copper stills and then finish off by taking a dram in the splendid Ships Room.

8 Highland Park
MAP A5 ■ Nr Kirkwall, Orkney
■ (01865) 885 604 ■ Tours: Apr–Oct daily; Nov–Mar Mon–Fri ■ Adm
■ www.highlandparkwhisky.com

Not the most famous whisky (though definitely among the

Macallan's whisky

TOP10 Places to Eat

Romantic interiors of The Witchery by the Castle

1 The Witchery by the Castle

Tucked away at the top of the Royal Mile, by Edinburgh Castle, it is hard to beat this restaurant (see p81) for its sheer theatricality and romantic appeal. The Secret Garden, enclosed in a courtyard, has a painted ceiling and a quiet terrace, while the main dining room is oak-panelled and full of rich tapestries.

2 Brian Maule at Chardon d'Or

Set in a Victorian townhouse with polished wooden floors, fresh flowers and candles in the evening, this is one of Glasgow's finest restaurants (see p101). Top quality beef, lamb and scallops, sourced from local suppliers, is prepared using French techniques. The menu features dishes such as rabbit roulade with roasted hazelnuts, grilled seabream with purple kale, and apple *tarte tatin* (caramelised fruit tart) with ice cream.

Delicious dessert at The Peat Inn

3 21212

Paul Kitching's Michelin-starred restaurant (see p81) delights gastronomes with an array of ever-changing, French influenced multi-course menus. There are paired wines to accompany each course.

4 The Cellar

Located in the fishing village of Anstruther, fresh fish is a speciality at this small, Michelin-starred restaurant (see p95). They offer a set menu and do not cater for vegan diets. Advance booking is essential.

5 The Peat Inn

Situated a short drive from the historic university town of St Andrews, this hotel's restaurant (see p95) is one of the most enduring and highly acclaimed places to eat in Scotland. Local produce is cooked in modern Scottish style. The menu includes roe deer with smoked swede puree, savoy cabbage, haggis and Madeira sauce.

6 The Kitchin

Run by celebrity chef Tom Kitchin, this restaurant (see p81) is set in a converted warehouse in Edinburgh's former docks. Scottish seasonal produce is lovingly prepared. There is even a creative vegetarian menu that features dishes such as sea kale salad and wild garlic and parsley risotto.

7 Three Chimneys

This iconic restaurant (see p127) in Skye, serves dishes designed to celebrate Scotland's culinary heritage. In addition to their main dining room, they have a "kitchen table" where guests can observe the chefs at work. It can seat eight people and can be reserved for exclusive use.

8 Knockinaam Lodge

Perched by the sea in Galloway, this acclaimed countryhouse hotel (see p89) offers gourmet dining. Expect some surprising combinations on the menu, such as roast chicken with a chicken and tarragon ravioli, mushroom puree and a cardamom and soya emulsion. Desserts might include a hot pistachio souffle with chocolate sauce.

Exterior of the Kinloch Lodge Hotel

9 Kinloch Lodge Hotel

It would be hard to beat this hotel's (see p127) idyllic setting, close to the water's edge in Sleat on the Isle of Skye. The food is equally delightful. The seven course tasting menu might feature Shetland cod with salt-baked beetroot.

10 The Silver Darling

Panoramic views of Aberdeen's beach are an attraction at this popular quayside restaurant (see p113). Scottish fish and shellfish are celebrated, with the menu featuring Shetland scallops, Loch Duart salmon and haddock from the North Sea.

TOP 10 SCOTTISH DISHES

Succulent venison ribs

1 Venison
The meat of wild red deer, dark and full-flavoured. It's served as a steak or cut into collops (slices of roast meat).

2 Haggis
Scotland's most famous dish is like a large, round sausage containing spiced sheep's offal, oats and seasoning. It is traditionally eaten at a Burn's supper with mashed "neeps" (swedes), "tatties" (potatoes) and a dram of whisky.

3 Rumbledethumps
Cabbage and onion braised in butter, mixed with mashed potatoes, topped with cheese and browned in the oven.

4 Stovies
A mix of potatoes, onions and beef cooked in the dripping (fat) from the Sunday roast.

5 Kippers
Fresh herring split open, salted and smoked. A common breakfast dish.

6 Arbroath Smokies
Similar to kippers, but these are smoked haddock rather than herring.

7 Smoked Salmon
Thin boneless slices of salmon that have been smoked to give a rich taste and deep pink colour.

8 Scotch Broth
A light soup made from mutton or beef stock, pearl barley and various vegetables such as carrots and leeks.

9 Cock-a-Leekie Soup
A warm, chunky soup of chicken, leeks, rice and prunes cooked in chicken stock – as wonderful as its name.

10 Cullen Skink
A Scottish version of chowder, this is a delicious soup made from smoked haddock, milk and mashed potato.

🔟 Scotland for Free

Scottish Parliament building, Edinburgh

1 Top Museums
All city museums in Glasgow and Edinburgh are free, so you won't have to pay to see many of the country's highlights, such as the National Museum of Scotland (see pp18–19), the Scottish National Gallery (see pp16–17) and Kelvingrove Art Gallery and Museum (see pp20–21).

2 Free Festival
www.freefestival.co.uk
Don't worry if you can't afford tickets to events in the Edinburgh Festival: the city is full of street performers in August, so just stroll around and enjoy the show. There is a free fringe programme too.

3 Holy Orders
Most of Scotland's churches are free to visit, including the historic St Giles' Cathedral in Edinburgh (see p14) and Glasgow Cathedral (see p97), though donations are welcome. Other churches include St Machar's Cathedral in Aberdeen.

Pictish carved stone

4 Seat of Power
Scotland's increasingly powerful Parliament (see p15) sits in a striking contemporary building at the foot of Edinburgh's Royal Mile. You can visit for a free guided tour (book in advance), which lasts for an hour and includes details about the architecture as well as the history of the Scottish Parliament. Book a free ticket to attend First Minister's Question Time.

5 Ancient Stones
Evidence of Neolithic peoples can be found at Calanais Standing Stones on Lewis (see p71) and Orkney's Ring of Brora (see p132). The Picts also left some visible reminders of their presence, like the mysterious carved stones and crosses around Aberlemno, near Glamis.

6 Wild at Heart
St Abbs Head National Nature Reserve, Eyemouth: (01890) 771 443; www.nts.org.uk ■ Scottish Dolphin Centre, Spey Bay: (01343) 820 339; open Apr–Oct:10:30am–5pm; www.dolphincentre.whales.org
Scotland's wildlife is rich and varied, and it doesn't have to cost you a penny to see it. St Abbs Head National Nature Reserve offers the chance to spot seabirds such as guillemots and razorbills. At the Scottish Dolphin Centre you can enjoy land-based dolphin watching.

Stained glass, St Giles' Cathedral

7 Glorious Garden

Entry is free to Glasgow's glorious Botanic Gardens *(see p49)*, which offer riverside walks and an arboretum, as well as stunning Victorian glasshouses, the most famous of which is the Kibble Palace *(see p99)*. There are fascinating guided walks in the summer.

8 Island Gin

www.lussagin.com

You can take a free tour of the wonderfully remote Lussa Gin Distillery on Jura. The gin is made using local botanicals such as bog myrtle and lemon thyme. Advance booking is recommended.

9 Ancient Trees

Scotland is home to some mighty trees that you can see for free. The most famous are the Birnam Oak in Dunkeld *(see p94)*, said to be the last survivor of Birnam Wood mentioned in Shakespeare's *Macbeth*; and the 3,000-year-old Fortingall Yew in Fortingall's churchyard – a contender for Britain's oldest tree, a short drive west of Pitlochry *(see p93)*.

The Birnam Oak, Dunkeld

10 Salmon Leap

MAP E4–5 ■ Pitlochry

On the Tummel in Pitlochry, you can watch salmon leaping up the specially constructed fish ladder, which by-passes a hydroelectric power station. It allows thousands of fish to complete their annual migration (Apr–Oct).

TOP 10 BUDGET TIPS

Road bridge to the Isle of Skye

1 Getting to the Isle
Use the free road bridge rather than the ferry to reach Skye.

2 Historic Scotland Explorer Passes
www.historicenvironment.scot
For five or fourteen days, gives free entry to over 70 properties.

3 VAT Refund
Non-EU visitors can reclaim the 20 per cent Value Added Tax (VAT) at participating stores.

4 National Trust for Scotland
www.nts.org.uk
Membership provides free entry to over 100 of their properties.

5 Spirit of Scotland Pass
www.scotrail.co.uk
A four- or eight-day Spirit of Scotland Pass gives free travel on railways and many ferries.

6 Cairngorms Golf Pass
www.visitcairngorms.com
A pass provides 30 per cent off green fees at any of 12 courses.

7 Wild Camping
www.outdooraccess-scotland.scot
Camp in the wild for free almost anywhere in the Scottish countryside.

8 Stay in a Bothy
www.mountainbothies.org.uk
Enjoy free, albeit simple accommodation maintained by The Mountain Bothies Association.

9 Sandemans New Europe
www.neweuropetours.eu
Sandemans offers free 2.5-hour walking tours of Edinburgh.

10 Stay in a Hostel
www.hostellingscotland.org
Many of Hostelling Scotland's hostels offer en-suite accommodation for families and couples, as well as dorm bunks.

🔟 Festivals and Events

Performer at the Celtic Connections festival

1 Music Festivals
www.celticconnections.com
- www.edinburghjazzfestival.com
- www.jazzfest.co.uk ▪ www.trnsmt
fest.com

Scotland offers up a diverse mix of musical events. Celtic Connections (Jan) is the world's largest festival of Celtic music. The summer sees both Edinburgh and Glasgow host jazz festivals, while TRNSMT festival on Glasgow Green welcomes big names like Stormzy and the Arctic Monkeys.

2 Sporting Events
www.sixnationsrugby.com
- www.braemargathering.org
- www.tireewaveclassic.co.uk

The Six Nations Rugby Tournament, held in early-spring, is the highlight of Scotland's sporting calendar. But there's plenty going on throughout the year, from Highland games such as the famous Braemar Gathering (Sep) to rural island surf festivals like the Tiree Wave Classic (Mar).

3 Whisky Galore
www.spiritofspeyside.com
- www.highlandwhiskyfestival.co.uk

May is Whisky Month, and whisky-themed events take place all over the country. The Spirit of Speyside Whisky Festival is a great opportunity to take part in tours and tastings in iconic distilleries. The Highland Whisky Festival showcases eight distilleries on the North Coast 500.

4 Foodie Favourites
www.fynefest.com
- www.tasteofgrampian.co.uk
- www.foodiesfestival.com

Scotland's summer food festivals champion local flavours. Sample Loch Fyne seafood, wild venison and over 200 ales at Fynefest. Celebrating East Coast produce is Inverurie's Taste of Grampian, a one-day flavour-fest that's easily worth the trip. For celebrity chef spotting, don't miss the Foodies Festival in Edinburgh.

5 On the Big Screen
www.edfilmfest.org.uk ▪ www.
glasgowfilm.org ▪ www.banff-uk.com
- www.lochnessfilmfestival.co.uk

The Edinburgh International Film Festival is the biggest name on Scotland's film scene, but events take place all over the country. Highlights include Glasgow Film Festival, Banff Mountain Film Festival and Loch Ness Film Festival.

6 Island Culture
www.stmagnusfestival.com
- www.seall.co.uk

The Orkney islands celebrate their patron saint with the St Magnus International Festival. Coinciding with midsummer, events usually include at least one world premiere of either music or drama, and feature some of the world's best musicians. Skye's Fèis an Eilein in early July celebrates island culture and music.

(7) Literary Events
www.edbookfest.co.uk
■ www.wigtownbookfestival.com

Charlotte Square plays host to the capital's summer showcase of bookish talent. It features best-selling authors for readings, debates and book signings. Held at the end of September in Scotland's National Book Town, Wigtown Book Festival may be small, but it packs a literary punch.

(8) Royal Edinburgh Military Tattoo
www.edintattoo.co.uk

Held every night during the month of August, the massive spectacle of the castle's Royal Edinburgh Military Tattoo parade is a swelling moment of national pride and vitality.

(9) Edinburgh International Festival and Fringe
www.eif.co.uk ■ www.edfringe.com

The greatest extravaganza of music, drama, dance and opera on the planet, the Edinburgh International Festival, which runs for the entirety of August, features the world's most prestigious performers, while the thousand-show Fringe brings the unknown and the avant-garde to the city.

Edinburgh Fringe Festival

(10) Hogmanay
No other nation in the world sees in the New Year with quite as much passion and pizzazz. Every Scottish town and city celebrates in their own way. Think all-night street parties, highland flings, pagan fire festivals or torchlight parades and, of course, plenty of fireworks.

TOP 10 SCOTTISH SHINDIGS

Up Helly Aa, Shetland

1 The Ba', Kirkwall
Wild ball game and energetic free-for-all played in the town's streets (Kirkwall, Orkney, 1 Jan).

2 Up Helly Aa
An incredible fire festival. Residents dress as Vikings and burn a replica longboat (late Jan, Shetland).

3 Borders Rugby Sevens
Skill, passion and mud. In rugby's heartland, each border town takes a day as host (Apr/May).

4 Burns An' A' That!
Scotland's top musical talent celebrates Scottish culture at venues around Ayrshire (late May).

5 Royal Highland Show
Over 150,000 people celebrate the biggest, best and most cultivated in the farming world (Jun, Edinburgh).

6 Pride Edinburgh
Scotland's national LGBTQ+ festival, with a traditional march through the city (mid-Jun).

7 Edinburgh International Jazz & Blues Festival
A rival to Glasgow's jazz event, this is the capital's own festival of cool music with venues across the city (Jul).

8 Speyfest
The best folk and traditional music performers gather at Fochabers, which is between Elgin and Buckie (late Jul).

9 World Pipe Band Championships
Astonishing sights and sounds as 3,000 pipers from around the world play on Glasgow Green (mid-Aug).

10 Hogmanay, Edinburgh
Internationally famed, Hogmanay is hosted at venues around the city, with live music and fireworks (31 Dec).

TOP 10 Island Attractions

Skara Brae, Orkney

1 Skara Brae, Orkney

The best-preserved group of prehistoric dwellings in Western Europe, this semi-subterranean village *(see p130)* is 5,000 years old and pre-dates both Egypt's pyramids and Stonehenge. The nine houses were linked by covered passageways and you can see their "fitted" stone furniture. Artifacts such as gaming dice and jewellery are displayed in the visitor centre.

2 Maeshowe, Orkney

It looks like a grassy mound from the outside, but stoop low and walk along its narrow entrance passage and you find yourself in a stunning, 5,000-year-old chambered grave *(see p130)*. After years of use it was closed, then rediscovered by Norse invaders – who left runic graffiti on the walls.

3 Islay's Distilleries

MAP G2–F2 ▪ www.islayinfo.com

They say that Irish monks introduced distilling to Islay in the 14th century. At one time there were over 20 distilleries on the island, producing its distinctive peat-smoked whisky. Now there are just nine, the most recent opened in 2018. The oldest, Bowmore, was first mentioned in 1779; the others are Ardbeg, Ardnahoe, Bruichladdich, Caol Ila, Bunnahbhain, Lagavulin, Laphroaig, and Kilchoman.

4 Iona Abbey and Nunnery

MAP F2 ▪ (01681) 700 512
▪ Open Apr–Sep: 9:30am–5:30pm daily; Oct–Mar: 10am–4pm Mon–Sat ▪ Adm ▪ www.historicenvironment. scot; www.welcometoiona.com

Iona has been a centre of Christian worship since AD 563, when St Columba founded his monastery here. It has been a pilgrimage site for hundreds of years. St Columba's shrine can be seen, as well as the 13th-century abbey church, and 8th-century stone crosses. It is said that Scottish kings and clan chiefs were buried here.

5 Fingal's Cave, Staffa

MAP E2 ▪ (01681) 700 659; www.nts.org.uk ▪ (01681) 700 755; www.staffatrips.co.uk

An Uamh Binn, or Cave of Melody, Fingal's Cave is a spectacular sea cave on the uninhabited island of Staffa. Its giant hexagonal columns and mystical beauty inspired Mendelssohn's *Hebrides Overture*, and featured in a painting by J M W Turner. Take a boat trip and see the island's fantastic wildlife such as basking sharks, seals and puffins.

Fingal's Cave, Staffa

6 The Italian Chapel, Orkney

MAP A5 ■ (01856) 781580 ■ Open
Jun–Aug: 9am–6:30pm daily (May &
Sep: to 5pm); Nov–Mar: 10am–1pm
daily (Apr & Oct: to 4pm) ■ Adm

Created from two
Nissen huts by Domenico
Chiocchetti and his fellow
Italian prisoners of war
between 1943 and 1944,
this church is their
memorial. Inside is
trompe l'oeil brickwork
and an altar made from
scrap; painted glass
windows depict St Francis
of Assisi. Truly a labour of love.

The Italian Chapel

7 Kinloch Lodge, Skye

Lovely atmosphere at the home
of Godfrey MacDonald, the chief of
the MacDonald clan *(see p43)*, and
his wife Claire, an acclaimed cookery writer. Bedrooms are individually
furnished, there are comfy sofas,
log fires, and fine food in the
restaurant *(see p127)*. There's
a cookery school, too.

8 Arran's Food Trail

MAP G3 ■ www.visitarran.com,
www.taste-of-arran.co.uk

The Isle of Arran *(see p126)* produces
a wonderful selection of food and
drink. Put together your own island
food trail by checking out its local

oatcakes, ice cream, haggis, black
pudding, cheeses, chocolate, whisky,
beer, smoked fish, preserves and
tablet (a bit like fudge, only harder
and sweeter).

9 Calanais Standing Stones, Lewis

MAP B2 ■ (01851) 621422
■ www.historicenviron
ment.scot, www.callanish
visitorcentre.co.uk

These magnificent
stones, arranged in
a cross shape with a
central circle, were erected around
5,000 years ago. Later, a chambered
tomb was added. Probably built as
an astronomical observatory by a
religious cult, they were abandoned
around 1,000 years later. There's
an informative exhibition in the
visitor centre (check the website
for opening hours).

Calanais Standing Stones, Isle of Lewis

10 Taransay

www.isleoftaransay.com

This little island is blessed with
stunning natural beauty, including
white-sand bays, machair grasslands
and heather-covered hills. Taransay
lacks a permanent human population,
but is home to a range of wildlife,
including golden eagles, seals and
red deer. The island became tempo-
rarily home to 30 "castaways", who
spent a year here as part of the BBC's
reality TV show *Castaway 2000*.

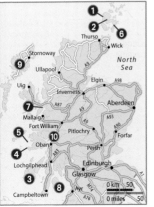

Scotland
Area by Area

The Dugald Stewart Monument
on top of Calton Hill, Edinburgh

 Edinburgh

With 18 golf courses, a dozen major parks, sufficient Neo-Classical architecture to dub it "the Athens of the North" and the crowning splendour of its castle, Edinburgh ranks as one of the world's most beautiful cities. Its centre is split in two: the historic Old Town, with its cobblestones and narrow wynds (alleys); and the striking Georgian architecture of the New Town. Between them lies Princes Street Gardens, a bowl of greenery in the heart of the bustle. No other city crams in as many festivals during the year as Edinburgh, and in August it becomes the greatest showcase on earth for comedy, music, drama, dance and every other conceivable form of culture.

National Museum of Scotland

EDINBURGH

Central Edinburgh

STOCKBRIDGE
BROUGHTON
NEW TOWN
Princes Street Gardens
OLD TOWN
WEST END

Waverley Station

Greater Edinburgh

Turnhouse Airport
Granton · Leith · Firth of Forth
Portobello
Gogar · Corstorphine · Sighthill · Morningside · Danderhall
Fairmilehead

Area of Central Edinburgh map

The Meadows
SOUTHS

LAURISTON PLACE
CRICHTON STREET
GEORGE SQUARE
MELVILLE DRIVE

0 km   5
0 miles 5

Edinburgh Castle on Castle Rock

1 Edinburgh Castle and the Royal Mile

This world-famous castle *(see pp12–13)* wears the nation's history. Here you'll find the Scottish Crown, Sword and Sceptre, and the legendary Stone of Destiny. The Royal Mile *(see pp14–15)* treads a straight but diverting path from the castle to Holyroodhouse.

2 Scottish National Gallery

Scotland's leading gallery *(see pp16–17)* includes masterpieces by the great Scottish artists, such as Raeburn and Ramsay, but is best known for its 15th- to 18th-century British and European paintings. In these collections, you'll find works by Botticelli, Velázquez, Raphael, Rembrandt, Rubens, Titian and many more besides.

3 National Museum of Scotland

Two adjoining buildings *(see pp18–19)* in radically different styles and with very diverse contents present the nation's most treasured historical artifacts. Worth visiting for the Lewis Chess Pieces alone, but don't expect to escape in under four hours.

4 Georgian House

MAP L3 ■ 7 Charlotte Square ■ 0131 225 2160 ■ Open Apr–Oct: 10am–5pm daily; Nov–Mar: 11am–4pm daily ■ Adm ■ www.nts.org.uk
A restored mansion on Charlotte Square, this is the best place to start a walking tour of the New Town. The area was the first daring adventure into planned architecture at a time of sordid living conditions for the masses. Begun in 1776, the beautifully proportioned buildings, set out in wide streets, crescents and squares, have lost none of their grandeur. Simply wander.

MONTGOMERY ST
HILLSIDE CRESCENT
OLD PL   LONDON ROAD
ROYAL TERRACE
10
CALTON
Regent Gardens
REGENT TERRACE ROAD
3
ABBEY HILL   ABBEYMOUNT
CALTON ROAD
7
CANONGATE
HORSE WYND
QUEEN'S DRIVE
CANONGATE
HOLYROOD ROAD   HOLYROOD GATE
5
COWGATE
QUEEN'S DRIVE
NEW STREET
Holyrood Park
PLEASANCE
Sailsbury Craig
DUMBIEDYKES
LEONARD'S STREET
CLERK STREET

0 metres 250
0 yards 250

Bedroom at Georgian House

5 Our Dynamic Earth

MAP R3 ■ Holyrood Rd ■ (0131) 550 7800 ■ Open Feb–Oct: 10am–5:30pm daily (Jul & Aug: to 6pm) ■ Adm ■ www.dynamicearth.co.uk

Every bit as exciting and illuminating for adults as it is for kids, Our Dynamic Earth (see p60) takes you on a journey through time and tells the story of planet Earth, from the Big Bang to the present. Amid this rapid evolution, environmental concerns are brought to the fore.

6 Royal Botanic Garden

MAP K5 ■ 20a Inverleith Row, Edinburgh ■ (0131) 248 2909 ■ Open Mar–Sep: 10am–6pm daily (Feb & Oct: to 5pm; Nov & Jan: to 4pm) ■ Adm for glasshouses ■ www.rbge.org.uk

Scotland's premier garden (see p48) with species from around the world. Lush greenhouses and glasshouses offer the perfect retreat on rainy days.

7 Holyroodhouse

Originally the abbey guesthouse, this was turned into a royal palace (see p15) by James IV of Scotland and is the Queen's official Scottish residence; she visits each summer. The Queen's Gallery is lined with portraits of Scottish royalty. The Royal Apartments are associated with Mary, Queen of Scots: it was here that David Rizzio, her Italian secretary, was brutally murdered on the orders of her husband, Lord Darnley. The Queen

PRINCES STREET GARDENS

An area of neutrality between New Town and Old, these lovely gardens shelter under the wing of the clifftop castle. During the Festival they become a major events venue, and throughout summer the famous Floral Clock, comprising over 2,000 plants, blooms in a corner by The Mound.

meets ministers and dignitaries in the State Apartments and the Throne Room is used for receptions and State occasions. In 1745, Bonnie Prince Charlie held extravagant balls in the Great Gallery and set up court in the palace for six weeks.

8 Calton Hill

MAP P2

Rising above the New Town with fantastic views, Calton Hill is home to a gathering of Classical buildings: the columned National Monument for the dead of the Napoleonic Wars, the Nelson Monument, commemorating the Battle of Trafalgar and the Old City Observatory.

Holyroodhouse

Visitors viewing modern art exhibits

⑨ Scottish National Gallery of Modern Art

MAP J3 ■ 75 Belford Rd ■ Open 10am–5pm daily (Aug: to 6pm) ■ www.nationalgalleries.org

Since it opened in 1960, this gallery has amassed some 5,000 post-1890 works. Here you can find the work of diverse figures such as Picasso, Munch, Charles Rennie Mackintosh and the Pop Art trio of Richard Hamilton, David Hockney and Jake Tilson. Also check out Modern Two opposite for contemporary shows.

The grand royal yacht *Britannia*

⑩ Royal Yacht Britannia

MAP K5 ■ Ocean Terminal, Leith ■ (0131) 555 5566 ■ Open Apr–Oct: 9:30am–4:30pm daily; Nov–Mar: 10am–3:30pm daily ■ Adm ■ www.royalyachtbritannia.co.uk

From 1953 to 1997 this was the Queen's floating home, the honey-mooning hotel of her children and Britain's roving royal court. Wander the decks of this fabulous ship with an audio tour that tells of the life and times of *Britannia*.

A DAY IN EDINBURGH

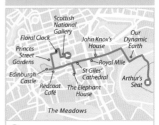

▶ MORNING

Start at the **Scottish National Gallery** *(see pp16–17)* at 10am. Ninety minutes should allow you to see the Botticelli, Canova and Raeburn's skating minister, the Rev Robert Walker, and far more.

Enter **Princes Street Gardens** at the Floral Clock (opposite the gallery), and ascend the path to **Edinburgh Castle** *(see pp12–13)*, taking care, as it's a steep climb.

Tour the castle, keeping an eye on your watch to make sure you're present when the dramatic One O'Clock Gun goes off. At the **Redcoat Café** *(Map M4; (0131) 225 9746; www.edinburghcastle.scot)*, have a platter to restore your energy levels before soldiering on.

AFTERNOON

Stroll down from the Castle Esplanade to the **Royal Mile** *(see pp14–15)*, stopping off at the **St Giles' Cathedral** *(see p14)* and probably several shops as well. Admire **John Knox's House** and have hot chocolate in **The Elephant House** *(Map N4; 21 George IV Bridge; (0131) 220 5355)* where the first of the Harry Potter books was written.

Turn right off the Royal Mile at Reid's Close (easy to miss) and visit **Our Dynamic Earth**, where you can pass several million years in a mere 2 hours or so.

If you still feel energetic, walk up the Salisbury Crags and **Arthur's Seat** for great evening views. Ninety minutes up and down (if you're fit) or grab a taxi and be driven most of the way up.

See map on pp74–5

The Best of the Rest

1 The Writers' Museum

Celebrating three great Scottish writers, Burns, Scott and Stevenson, The Writers' Museum *(see p14)* has rare books and items such as Burns' writing desk. There is Stevenson's wardrobe, made by the infamous Deacon Brodie, who was the inspiration behind *The Strange Case of Dr Jekyll and Mr Hyde*.

The Writers' Museum sign

2 Scottish National Portrait Gallery

MAP N2 ■ Queen St ■ www.national-galleries.org

Marvel at more than 3,000 portraits of famous Scots, including Robert Burns and Bonnie Prince Charlie.

3 St Giles' Cathedral

The Scottish Reformation was launched by John Knox in this church *(see p14)*. Attractions include the Thistle Chapel and memorials to Robert Burns and R L Stevenson.

4 Greyfriars Kirk

MAP N4 ■ Greyfriars Pl ■ Adm■ www.greyfriarskirk.com

Historic church, best known for the grave of John Gray, owner of "Greyfriars Bobby" (1858–72), a devoted terrier who lived by his master's grave. A statue of this faithful dog stands outside the cemetery.

5 Surgeons' Hall Museums

MAP P4 ■ Nicolson St ■ Adm ■ www.museum.rcsed.ac.uk

Appreciating Edinburgh's contribution to surgery, this group of three adjoining museums covers everything, including the history of pathology, midwifery and dentistry.

6 Hopetoun

MAP J5 ■ Sth Queensferry ■ Adm ■ www.hopetoun.co.uk

This architectural gem built by the industrious Robert Adam, is both a stately home of the Earls of Hopetoun and an art treasury (paintings by Canaletto, Rubens, Rembrandt, to name but a few).

7 Real Mary King's Close

MAP N3 ■ 2 Warriston's Cl, High St ■ (0131) 225 0672 ■ Adm ■ www.realmarykingsclose.com

Shiver as you tour this warren of streets hidden beneath the City Chambers. Closed off after the 1645 plague, they are said to be haunted.

8 Lauriston Castle

Davidson's Mains ■ (0131) 336 2060 ■ Adm ■ www.edinburgh museums.org.uk

This Edwardian mansion features a 16th-century tower house, lovely grounds, and fine furniture and antiques. Admission by tour only.

9 Scottish Mining Museum

Newtongrange ■ (0131) 663 7519 ■ Adm ■ www.nationalmining museum.com

Don your headlamp for an enlightening underground tour.

10 Scotch Whisky Experience

MAP M4 ■ Castlehill ■ (0131) 220 0441 ■ Adm ■ www.scotchwhisky experience.co.uk

A replica distillery with the world's largest collection of Scotch whisky.

Places to Shop

1 Edinburgh Books
MAP M4 ▪ 145 West Port

One of many independent bookshops, to the west of Grassmarket, sells new and second-hand books. West Port's selection focuses on the arts.

2 Hector Russell
MAP N3–4 ▪ 137-141 High St

Made-to-measure kilts and a gathering of the tartans. They offer kilts for hire too.

3 Armstrongs
MAP N4 ▪ 81–83 Grassmarket

A fabulous pre-loved clothing store that is filled with half a century's worth of vintage apparel and footwear. Find everything from velvet jackets to cowboy boots, kilts to dresses.

4 Halibut & Herring
MAP L6 ▪ 108 Bruntsfield Place

Find Scottish handmade soaps here and all manner of colourful, squeezy and bathroom accessories, in aquatic hues. It is a useful stop to buy gifts.

5 Edinburgh Printmakers
Castle Mills, 1 Dundee St

On display here are a range of limited-edition works from contemporary printmakers at reasonable prices.

6 I J Mellis
MAP N4 ▪ 30A Victoria St

I J Mellis's cheeses are celebrated all around Scotland, and feature in many Edinburgh menus, but the Victoria Street branch goes beyond to embrace a panoply of culinary delicacies. Stock your picnic hamper here.

Scotch Whisky on display, Royal Mile

7 Royal Mile Whiskies
MAP N4 ▪ 379 High St

A cornucopia of all things alcoholic, particularly single malt Scotch whisky, with hundreds of varieties on offer and regular tasting sessions.

8 St James Quarter
MAP P2 ▪ Picardy Place/ Multrees Walk

This vast multi-storey mall opened in 2021 and is filled with high-end clothing, jewellery and accessory brands, as well as countless bars, cafés and restaurants.

9 Edinburgh Farmers' Market
MAP L4 ▪ Castle Terrace

The city's weekly foodie fest spreads its wares beneath the castle crags every Saturday morning, selling everything from Scottish cheeses and venison sandwiches, to local craft beers and traditional Scottish sweets.

10 Tiso Edinburgh
MAP M3 ▪ 123 Rose St
▪ Leith branch: 41 Commercial St

An outdoor clothing and gear shop, Tiso Edinburgh has everything you need before heading for the hills. The Leith branch also offers a café and a ski servicing centre.

Cheeses at I J Mellis

See map on pp74–5

Bars and Pubs

1 Bow Bar
MAP N4 ■ 80 West Bow St

Lush red and cream gloss paintwork envelops this modest pub, where the background sounds are the jovial chatter and clinking glasses.

2 The Blue Blazer
MAP L5 ■ 2 Spittal St

Perfect for discerning drinkers, this place offers real ales and an array of malt whiskies. The back room hosts regular live folk-music sessions.

3 Bennet's
MAP L6 ■ 8 Leven St

This classic old-school pub, with its ornate interior and superb portfolio of malt whiskies, real ales and fancy cocktails, is one of a vanishing breed.

4 Dome Bar
MAP M2 ■ 14 George St

Dome Bar is a Corinthian-columned whale of a building, entered through a flight of steps flanked by nocturnal doormen. Its interiors are decorated with chandeliers and palm plants. There are many bars and dining areas such as the Georgian Tea Room and the majestic Grill Room. The Front Bar is great for cocktails.

Lavish interior of Dome Bar

Craft beer bar, BrewDog

5 BrewDog
MAP N4 ■ 143 Cowgate

Scotland's most successful artisan brewery operates this industrial-chic altar to craft beer, a hugely popular oasis of real ales in the Old Town.

6 City Café
MAP P4 ■ 19 Blair St

Ideally situated in the heart of the city's clubland, this popular bar packs in the capital's contingent of party people on weekend nights.

7 Bramble
MAP M2 ■ 16a Queen St

Stone steps lead down to this maze-like, candlelit cellar where accomplished mixologists create some of Edinburgh's finest cocktails.

8 Café Royal Circle Bar
MAP N2 ■ 19 West Register St

Walk in at lunchtime to swirling ceilings, brass lamps and a convivial atmosphere of both young and old, enjoying simple seafood dishes from the kitchen of the Oyster Bar next door.

9 Joseph Pearce
MAP P1 ■ 23 Elm Row, Leith Walk

Swedish owners have taken this century-old Scottish pub and given it a Scandinavian makeover, creating a welcoming and family-friendly bar.

10 The Cumberland
MAP M1 ■ 1–3 Cumberland St

Enjoy the well-lit, cosy interiors of this much-loved pub in the winter, or cool down in its side garden in the summer.

Places to Eat

PRICE CATEGORIES

For a three-course meal for one with half a bottle of wine (or equivalent meal), taxes and extra charges.

£ under £30   ££ £30–60   £££ over £60

1 **Chez Jules**
MAP M2 ▪ 109 Hanover St
▪ (0131) 226 6992 ▪ £

This cheerful, little bistro serves classic French dishes such as *moules frites* and *aioli* and beef bourguignon; the lunchtime set menu has terrific value.

2 **The Witchery by the Castle**
MAP M4 ▪ Castlehill ▪ (0131) 225 5613 ▪ ££

Aim for the Secret Garden room to experience The Witchery *(see p64)* at its romantic best. It excels at dishes with a rural flavour. Try the foraged soup, roast wood pigeon, loin of venison.

3 **Restaurant Martin Wishart**
MAP K5 ▪ 54 The Shore, Leith ▪ (0131) 553 3557 ▪ £££

Make sure to book ahead for this Michelin-starred restaurant. The food is memorable and the lunch is of excellent value.

4 **Timberyard**
MAP M4 ▪ 10 Lady Lawson St ▪ (0131) 221 1222 ▪ £££

Originality is the watchword at this beautifully converted wood-working shop. The focus is on locally produced seafood, pork and game garnished with foraged ingredients, such as damsons and mustard leaf.

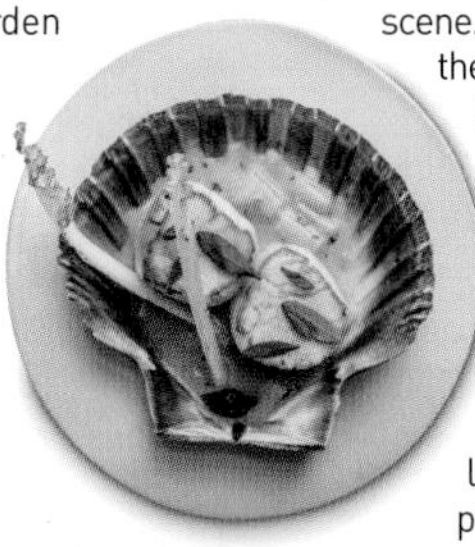

French cuisine, The Kitchin

5 **Fishers, Leith**
1 The Shore, Leith; (0131) 554 5666 ▪ Fishers in the City (sister restaurant): MAP M2; 58 Thistle St ▪ ££

This seafood restaurant is loved for its honed cooking and warm ambience.

6 **The Scran and Scallie**
MAP K1 ▪ 1 Comely Bank Rd ▪ www.scranandscallie.com ▪ ££

This upscale gastro-pub, managed by star chef Tom Kitchin, serves modern classics based on Scottish produce.

7 **The Kitchin**
MAP F5 ▪ 78 Commercial Quay ▪ (0131) 555 1755 ▪ £££

Tom Kitchin's Michelin-starred restaurant *(see p64)* has made a startling impact on the country's culinary scene. Sample some of the exemplary French-influenced cuisine here.

8 **Ondine**
MAP N4 ▪ 2 George IV Bridge ▪ (0131) 226 1888 ▪ £££

Seafood, from Scottish lobster to Portuguese prawns via Breton shellfish, graces the menu at this sleek and sophisticated restaurant.

9 **The Little Chartroom**
MAP K5 ▪ 14 Bonnington Rd ▪ (0131) 556 6600 ▪ www.thelittle chartroom.com ▪ ££

This tiny restaurant, popular with diners, offers innovative dishes like octopus carpaccio and lamb with courgette and merguez.

10 **21212**
MAP Q2 ▪ 3 Royal Terrace ▪ (0131) 523 1030 ▪ www.21212 restaurant.co.uk ▪ ££

Paul Kitching presides over a Michelin-starred contemporary fine-dining restaurant *(see p64)* featuring a French-influenced menu.

See map on pp74–5

🔟 Southern Scotland

A beautiful region of abrupt and rolling hills, sheep pastures, forested valleys and slow-moving rivers, Southern Scotland is the home of rugby, Robert Burns, Sir Walter Scott and spectacular castles and abbeys. For centuries this border country was the flashpoint of hostility between Scotland and England, but also a centre of commerce and religion. The monuments of these times represent some of the best medieval and Renaissance architecture in Europe. The border towns contest their rugby reputations in winter and, with equal passion, celebrate ancient riding festivals in summer.

Burns Monument, Alloway

SOUTHERN SCOTLAND

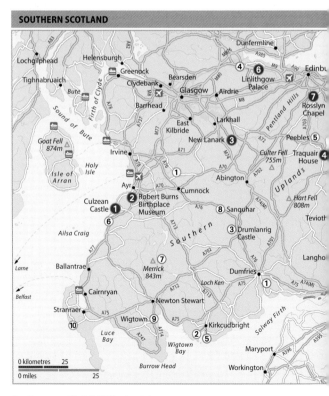

0 kilometres   25
0 miles   25

Previous pages The Falkirk Wheel at night

1 Culzean Castle

This cliff-edge castle *(see pp32–3)* was remodelled into a magnificent home for the Earls of Cassillis in 1777 by Georgian architectural master Robert Adam.

2 Robert Burns Birthplace Museum

MAP G4 ■ Murdoch's Lone, Alloway ■ (01292) 443 700 ■ Open 10am–5pm (cottage: 11am–3:30pm) ■ Adm (free for NTS members) ■ www.nts.org.uk

The world's finest collection of Burnsian memorabilia and manuscripts can be found in this museum. The cottage where the poet was born and spent the first seven years of his life is also nearby. The heritage park includes the Burns Monument and the Brig o'Doon bridge.

New Lanark on the River Clyde

3 New Lanark

MAP G4 ■ (01555) 661 345 ■ Open 11am–4pm Fri–Mon ■ Adm ■ www.newlanark.org

In 1820, at the height of the Industrial Revolution, factory owner Robert Owen recognized the need for safe and efficient working conditions, matched by good-quality housing for his workers. New Lanark was the result, a modern industrial town that also comprised an education system (including the world's first nursery school) and free healthcare. Now a UNESCO World Heritage Site, this living museum is still pioneering.

4 Traquair House

MAP G5 ■ Innerleithen ■ (01896) 830 323 ■ Opening times vary, check website ■ Adm ■ www.traquair.co.uk

Atmospheric Traquair dates back to 1107 and is Scotland's oldest inhabited house. The interior includes a hidden room leading to secret stairs along which Catholic priests could escape during persecutions. Both Mary Queen of Scots and Bonnie Prince Charlie have stayed here.

5 Manderston House

MAP F6 ■ Duns ■ (01361) 883 450 ■ House and gardens: open Apr–Sep on selected dates for tours only; check website for details ■ Adm ■ www.manderston.com

This stunning and massive Edwardian mansion features a lake and woodland. It was built to impress Scottish society. The most lavish feature of the interior is the silver staircase; there are also fine artworks and antiques.

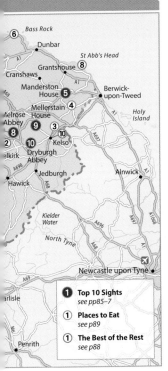

Mary Queen of Scots

6 Linlithgow Palace

MAP F5 ■ Linlithgow ■ (01506) 842896 ■ Closed for restoration ■ Adm ■ www.historic environment.scot

One of only four royal palaces in Scotland, Linlithgow was the birthplace of Mary Queen of Scots and provided a temporary safe haven for Bonnie Prince Charlie during the Jacobite Rebellion (see p38). Solid and fortress-like on the banks of Linlithgow Loch, the palace still looks majestic in its semi-ruined state. This was the finest building of its day, and its master masons have left a wealth of carvings. Look around the Great Hall and chapel and marvel at the expertise of the craftsmen who laboured upon this wonderful building.

7 Rosslyn Chapel

MAP F5 ■ Rosslyn ■ (0131) 440 2159 ■ Open 9am–5pm daily (last adm 3:40pm) ■ Adm ■ www. rosslynchapel.com

As extraordinary as it is mysterious, you'd be hard pushed to cram more carvings into such a small place. Built in 1446, it has a great variety of styles and subjects. Most curious of all are

Intricate carvings in Rosslyn Chapel

the carvings of North American plants, which predate Columbus's transatlantic voyage of discovery by 100 years. The chapel has become extremely popular since featuring in the book and film *The Da Vinci Code*.

8 Melrose Abbey

MAP G5 ■ Melrose ■ (01896) 822562 ■ Grounds, cloister and museum: open Apr–Sep: 10am–5pm daily (Oct–Mar: to 4pm); Abbey church: closed for restoration ■ Adm ■ www.historicenvironment.scot

The tall lancet windows of this ruin must have appeared miraculous to medieval worshippers. Founded in 1136 by David I, this was the first Cistercian monastery in Scotland. It was rebuilt in the 1380s having suffered due to border conflicts, but faced further damage in the 16th century. It now stands as a beleaguered but romantic spot for the ghost of Robert the Bruce, whose heart is believed to reside here.

Melrose Abbey

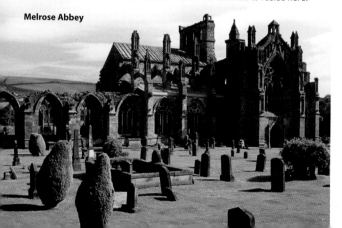

9 **Mellerstain House**
MAP G6 ■ Gordon ■ (01573) 410225 ■ Open May–Sep: 12:30–5pm Fri–Mon ■ Adm ■ www.mellerstain.com

Scotland's most splendid Georgian house (early 18th century) is another creation by architect Robert Adam. This vast edifice of perfect symmetry on the outside has rooms of perfect proportions within. The delicate plasterwork of the library, resembling fine china, is considered one of Adam's greatest accomplishments. Exquisite details abound throughout the interior, while outside, grand terraced gardens run down to an ornamental lake.

Façade of Mellerstain House

10 **Dryburgh Abbey**
MAP G6 ■ Nr St Boswells ■ (01835) 822381 ■ Closed for restoration ■ Adm (free for HES members) ■ www.historicenvironment.scot

Located on a bend in the River Tweed, these are the most beautiful and evocative ruins in southern Scotland. Founded in 1152, the abbey was destroyed by the English in 1322, 1344 and again in 1385, but each time it rose to magnificence once more, until it was finally consumed by fire in 1544. Despite having lain in ruin for 500 years, it is remarkably complete, and the quality of masonry is unbelievable. See it when shadows fall for the most spectacular views.

A TOUR OF THE BORDERS

▶ MORNING

Shop at the **Edinburgh Farmers' Market** or **I J Mellis** (see p79) the day before your trip to make a gourmet picnic – as simple or as lavish as you like.

The next morning, set off early to avoid the 9am rush hour, and drive to **Rosslyn Chapel** to see the extraordinary carvings. Tear yourself away from this magical spot, and drive on to Penicuik and take the A703 to Peebles. It's worth having a break for coffee in this pretty town.

Now take the lovely Tweedside A72, then bear off onto the B7062 to reach **Traquair House** (see p85). Explore this fascinating building, which is still home to the Maxwell-Stuart family, then enjoy lunch at one of the picnic tables in the extensive grounds.

AFTERNOON

Return to the A72, then continue to visit either **Abbotsford House** (see p88), the home of Sir Walter Scott, or drive a bit further to the romantic ruins of **Dryburgh Abbey**, where the great writer is buried. Both properties are a short drive from Scott's View, from where you can see the Eildon Hills, and its distinctive three peaks, while you delve once more into your picnic hamper for afternoon tea.

Return to Edinburgh for your evening meal, or continue to explore the Borders at your leisure and enjoy the stunning scenery.

See map on pp84–5 ←

The Best of the Rest

The stunning Caerlaverock Castle

1 Caerlaverock Castle

MAP H5 ■ 13 km (8 miles) SE of Dumfries on the B725 ■ (01387) 770 244 ■ Closed for restoration ■ Adm (free for HES members) ■ www.historicenvironment.scot

Still remarkably complete, despite having been ruined for over 400 years, this moated triangular castle is a stunning sight.

2 Abbotsford House

MAP G5 ■ Nr Melrose ■ (01896) 752 043 ■ Open Mar & Nov: 10am–4pm daily (Apr–Oct: to 5pm) ■ Adm ■ www.scottsabbotsford.com

Home of the great novelist Sir Walter Scott, crammed with historical bric-a-brac. A short drive away on the B6356 is Scott's View.

3 Drumlanrig Castle

MAP G4 ■ Thornhill, Dumfries and Galloway ■ (01848) 331 555 ■ Castle: open Easter, May bank holidays, Jul & Aug: 11am–4pm ■ Grounds: Apr–Sep: open 10am–5pm ■ Adm ■ www.drumlanrigcastle.co.uk

With a priceless collection of art and Jacobite treasures, this 1676 castle is home to the Duke of Buccleuch.

4 Falkirk Wheel

MAP F4 ■ Falkirk ■ (08700) 500 208 ■ Visitor centre: open 10am–5:30pm daily ■ Adm (for boat trips) ■ www.scottishcanals.co.uk

An engineering first, the world's only rotating boat lift was conceived with the intention of linking the Union and Forth and Clyde canals. Book a boat trip to soak in the views.

5 Kirkcudbright

MAP H4 ■ Dumfries and Galloway ■ www.kirkcudbright.town

Pronounced "kirkoobree", this fishing port and artists' colony offers a ruined castle, a gallery and arts centre, plus Broughton House, one time home of artist E A Cornel.

6 Scottish Seabird Centre

MAP F5 ■ North Berwick ■ (01620) 890 202 ■ Open Nov–Jan: 10am–4pm daily (Apr–Aug: to 6pm; Feb, Mar, Sep & Oct: to 5pm) ■ Adm ■ www.seabird.org

Remote cameras relay live action from the Bass Rock's 100,000 gannets. Take time for a boat trip (see p61).

7 Galloway Forest Park

MAP H4 ■ www.forestryandland.gov.scot

Area of superb loch, forest and hill scenery. Picnic at Bruce's Stone or have a day out on foot or on bikes.

8 St Abb's Head

MAP F6 ■ Visitor centre: (01890) 771 443; open Apr–Oct: 10am–5pm daily

A national nature reserve on dramatic cliffs packed with birds. Don't miss the characterful town of St Abb's with its fishery museum.

9 Wigtown

MAP H4 ■ www.wigtown-booktown.co.uk

Scotland's designated book town with many bookshops and a fantastic literary festival held each September

10 Floors Castle

MAP G6 ■ Kelso ■ (01573) 223 333 ■ Open May–Sep: 10:30am–5pm daily (Oct–Mar: grounds and gardens only) ■ Adm ■ www.floorscastle.com

This magnificent property, built in 1721 for the first Duke of Roxburghe, is still the family home.

Places to Eat

PRICE CATEGORIES
For a three-course meal for one with half a bottle of wine (or equivalent meal), taxes and extra charges.

£ under £30 ££ £30–60 £££ over £60

1 Sorn Inn
MAP G4 ■ 35 Main St, Sorn, Ayrshire ■ (01290) 551 305 ■ Closed Mon–Tue ■ ££

Family-friendly country pub serving quality classics such as steak pie, roast chicken and haddock and chips.

2 Castle Street Bistro
MAP H4 ■ 5 Castle St, Kirkcudbright ■ (01557) 330 569 ■ ££

Cosy bistro offering Scots-French influenced cuisine such as duck breast with orange and cointreau.

3 Cobbles Inn
MAP G6 ■ 7 Bowmont St, Kelso ■ (01573) 223 548 ■ ££

Popular town-centre gastropub offering bar lunches, fine dining in the evening, and craft beers from the nearby Tempest microbrewery.

4 Wheatsheaf at Swinton
MAP G6 ■ The Green, Swinton ■ (01890) 860 257 ■ ££

Local lamb, fish and game are on the menu at this smart, country-style restaurant with a lovely setting overlooking the village green.

5 Peebles Hydro
MAP G5 ■ Innerleithen Rd, Peebles ■ (01764) 651 846 ■ ££

The changing menu at this smart hotel restaurant features mouthwatering dishes such as crusted cod loin and braised pork belly, with desserts such as pear and blackberry crumble.

6 Wildings Restaurant
MAP G4 ■ Harbour Rd, Maidens, Ayrshire ■ (01655) 331 401 ■ ££

An attractive restaurant with Isle of Arran views, and a seasonal menu using local ingredients.

7 Marmions
MAP G5 ■ 5 Buccleuch St, Melrose ■ (01896) 822 245 ■ Closed Sun ■ ££

Long-running French-style brasserie, popular with both locals and visitors. Snacks, an à la carte menu and wines for all tastes.

8 Blackaddie Country House Hotel
MAP G4 ■ Sanquhar ■ (01659) 50270 ■ £££

A classy restaurant serving modern Scottish dishes made from quality local produce.

9 Windlestraw
MAP G5 ■ Galashiels Rd, Walkerburn, Borders ■ (01896) 870 636 ■ www.windlestraw.com ■ ££

Set in a historic house, this restaurant features a kitchen garden that provides many of chef Stuart Waterston's menu ingredients. Try the borders lamb and game or the seafood from nearby fishing ports.

10 Knockinaam Lodge
MAP H3 ■ Portpatrick ■ (01776) 810 471 ■ £££

Traditional food with a modern touch in a sumptuous country house (see p65). Memorable seafood, such as a simple dish of pan-seared scallops. A five-course tasting menu offers the best of the kitchen.

Picturesque Knockinaam Lodge

See map on pp84–5

🔟 North and East of Edinburgh

A two-hour drive from the centre of Edinburgh takes you either into the majestic Highland-like landscape of Perthshire, or through the rich farmland of Fife, with its coastal fringe of pretty seaside villages.

Quaint cottages in Culross

This area is Scotland arguably at its most diverse, with famous castles, abbeys, ships, bridges, wildlife reserves and golf courses all found within easy reach of each other by car. Golf is Scotland's greatest sporting tradition, and it is much in evidence here – especially in St Andrews, the sport's original home. The many castles and palaces are testament to the enduring appeal of this pleasing and photogenic region.

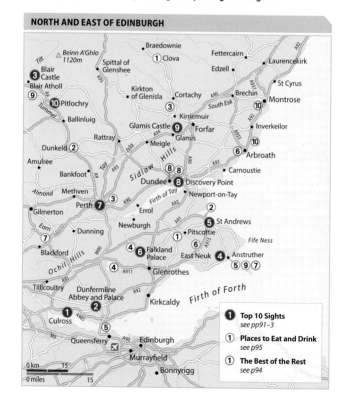

NORTH AND EAST OF EDINBURGH

1 **Top 10 Sights**
see pp91–3

1 **Places to Eat and Drink**
see p95

1 **The Best of the Rest**
see p94

1 Culross

MAP F5 ■ Palace: (01383) 880 359; open Apr–Sep: 10am–5pm daily (Oct: to 4pm Fri–Mon) ■ Adm (free for NTS members) ■ www.nts.org.uk

Once a thriving village with mines, iron workings and trade links with the Low Countries, Culross fell into decline in the 18th and 19th centuries. Its restoration began in the 1930s, and now the town is a striking resurrection of its 16th- and 17th-century heyday.

2 Dunfermline Abbey and Palace

MAP F5 ■ Dunfermline ■ (01383) 723 005 ■ Open Apr–Sep: 9:30am–5:30pm daily; Oct–Mar: 10am–4pm Sat–Wed ■ Adm ■ www.dunfermlineabbey.com

Founded in the 11th century by Queen (later St) Margaret *(see p13)*, the abbey's stunning feature is the 12th-century Romanesque nave. This was the burial place of Robert the Bruce – without his heart, which he requested be taken on a Crusade to the Holy Land. A skeleton with the heart chamber cut open was discovered in a grave here in 1818; the site is now marked by a plaque to honour the key figure of the Battle of Bannockburn *(see p38)*.

3 Blair Castle

MAP E4 ■ Blair Atholl ■ (01796) 481 207 ■ Open 10am–5pm daily ■ Adm ■ www.atholl-estates.co.uk/blair-castle

This striking castle is the ancestral seat of the Duke of Atholl. Dating from 1269, it has been extended

Blair Castle and the hills of Perthshire

over the centuries and is embellished with crenellations, turrets and a grand ballroom. Queen Victoria was so impressed when she stayed that she gave the then Duke permission to raise a private army. On the hour, one of the Highlander pipers plays in front of the castle.

4 East Neuk

MAP F5–6

Neuk is a Scots word for "corner", and the East Neuk refers to a small bend in the coastline along which is found a remarkable chain of picturesque fishing villages. They run from Earlsferry to Crail, and every one is a gem. Elie and Crail are probably the most quaint and are favoured haunts of artists. Pittenweem's beautiful harbour is still a working port, and Anstruther, a haven for yachts, has a bustling seafront. The latter is also home to the excellent Scottish Fisheries Museum *(see p94)*.

Yachts docked at the busy harbour in Anstruther

The ruins of St Andrews Cathedral

5 St Andrews

MAP F5 ■ Cathedral & Castle: open Apr–Sep: 9:30am–5:30pm daily, Oct–Mar: 10am–4pm daily; adm ■ Golf courses: (01334) 466 666; www.standrews.com

The "home of golf" *(see p56)* has the oldest university in Scotland, and red-robed students add a colourful, carefree atmosphere to this town. St Andrews was once the ecclesiastical capital of the country and its cathedral is still a proud ruin. Its castle has unrivalled examples of siege tunnels and a curious "bottle dungeon". There's also a long beach for walks, and plenty of hip cafés and bistros.

HOME OF GOLF

The coastal links courses around St Andrews are recognized as the birthplace of golf – the earliest record of the game being played here dates to 1457. Golfing heritage continues in the city to this day, and St Andrew's Royal and Ancient Golf Club remains the ruling arbiter of the game.

6 Falkland Palace

MAP F5 ■ Falkland ■ (0133) 785 7397 ■ Open Mar–May & Sep–Oct: 11am–5pm Mon–Sat (Jun–Aug: from 10am Mon–Sat, from noon Sun) ■ Adm (free for NTS members) ■ www.nts.org.uk

A sense of history pervades this palace, the home of Mary Queen of Scots and the Stuart kings from 1541. Restored royal bedchambers and fine 17th-century tapestries are on display. Most intriguing is the oldest

Falkland Palace crest

real tennis court still in use in Britain, built in 1539. Unlike the modern game, real tennis was played indoors and is similar to squash.

7 Perth and Scone Palace

MAP E5 ■ Palace: (01738) 552 300; open May–Sep: 9:30am–5pm (Apr & Oct: 10am–5pm); adm ■ Grounds: Nov–Mar: open 10am–4pm Fri–Sun ■ Adm ■ www.scone-palace.co.uk

Known as the "Fair City", Perth is situated on the tree-lined River Tay. Its streets are a delight of small shops for browsing. North of the city, off the A93, is Scone Palace. The grounds contain the Moot Hill, where Scottish kings were crowned on the famous Stone of Destiny *(see p12)*, now in Edinburgh Castle.

(8) Discovery Point

MAP E5 ■ Dundee ■ (01382) 309 060 ■ Open Apr–Oct: 10am–6pm daily (from 11am Sun); Nov–Mar: 10am–5pm daily (from 11am Sun) ■ Adm ■ www. rrsdiscovery.co.uk

The chill and hazards of Antarctic exploration grip you in this hi-tech exhibition. Focusing on the expeditions of Shackleton and Scott, this display uses original film footage, modern images and interactive computer screens. Tour the Dundee-built boat RSS *Discovery*, that carried Scott and his companions on their ill-fated expedition. While in Dundee visit the Contemporary Arts Centre on Nethergate for great exhibitions and its fine café-bar.

(9) Glamis Castle

MAP E5 ■ Glamis, Angus ■ (01307) 840 393 ■ Open 10am–4pm daily ■ Adm ■ www.glamis-castle.co.uk

A royal residence since 1372, this magical castle (see p40) with towers, turrets and treasures has a link with Shakespeare's *Macbeth*.

Interiors of the Glamis Castle

(10) Pitlochry

MAP E4–5 ■ Theatre: (01796) 484 626 ■ Information Centre: 22 Atholl Rd; open 9:30am–5:30pm Mon–Sat, 10am–4pm Sun (shorter hours in winter, longer in summer) ■ www.pitlochryfestivaltheatre.com

This tartan-and-tweed town has a long history of serving visitors. Its proximity to Perthshire's beauty spots and sporting estates was the original draw, but now its major attractions are a fine theatre and a fish ladder, where salmon leap up a series of pools to reach spawning grounds.

AN EAST COAST DRIVE

▶ MORNING

Leave Edinburgh around 9am and make for South Queensferry to photograph the iconic **Forth Bridges** (see p94). There's an information centre where you can find out about the history of the bridges, and about the Queensferry Crossing.

Cross the road bridge and take the M90 to **Perth**. Stroll around the town, have a coffee, then follow the A93 to **Scone Palace** to see where Scottish kings such as Macbeth and Robert the Bruce were crowned. If you're hungry, have lunch here; they source ingredients from the palace kitchen garden.

Now it's about an hour's drive, via the A90 to Dundee where you can stop at **Discovery Point** and shiver at the exploits of the Antarctic explorers. Otherwise cross the Tay Bridge, then join the A919 to reach **St Andrews**, home to Scotland's oldest university and most famous golf course. There are plenty of places to eat.

AFTERNOON

You could easily spend the rest of the day strolling around St Andrews' quaint streets, but if you continue along the coast you'll come to the East Neuk fishing villages of Crail and Pittenweem (see p91) – not forgetting lovely Anstruther, where you'll find the Scottish Fisheries Museum (see p94). Relax, soak up the scenery and enjoy a meal in one of the excellent fish restaurants (see p95).

See map on p90 ←

The Best of the Rest

① Hill of Tarvit Mansion

MAP F5 ■ Cupar ■ (01334) 653 127 ■ House: open Apr–Oct: 11am–4pm Sat & Sun (tours until noon) ■ Grounds: open 9am–dusk daily ■ Adm (free for NTS members) ■ www.nts.org.uk

This 17th-century mansion with vast grounds was remodelled in 1904 for a wealthy industrialist. It features cutting edge technology with electricity, telephones and central heating.

② Dunkeld

MAP E5

A village of great charm and character, with the noble ruins of its 14th-century cathedral and gorgeous riverside walks.

③ Kirriemuir and the Angus Glens

MAP E5

J M Barrie, creator of Peter Pan, was born in Kirriemuir; his birthplace is now a museum. Nearby are the wild and beautiful Angus Glens, great for scenic hikes.

Statue of Peter Pan, Kirriemuir

④ Loch Leven

MAP F5 ■ Adm

Mary, Queen of Scots, was imprisoned in this ruined castle. The loch provides a haven for birds – including ospreys.

⑤ Forth Bridges

MAP F5

The iconic cantilever rail bridge, suspension road bridge and the striking Queensferry Crossing are best seen lit up at night.

⑥ Arbroath Abbey

MAP E6 ■ (01241) 878 756 ■ Closed for restoration ■ Adm (free for HES members)

The abbey makes for impressive ruins, but it's known for the copy of the "Declaration of Arbroath", Scotland's eloquent charter for independence.

⑦ Scottish Fisheries Museum

MAP F5 ■ Anstruther ■ (01333) 310 628 ■ Adm ■ www.scotfish museum.org

It's hard to believe just how fascinating boats, nets and fish can be. This museum offers a first-class overview of the history of the fish supper.

⑧ Verdant Works

MAP E5 ■ Dundee ■ (01382) 309 060 ■ Adm ■ www.verdantworks.co.uk

Set in a refurbished mill, this is an invigorating presentation of the jute industry, the material upon which Dundee founded its urban economy.

⑨ Killiecrankie

MAP E4–5 ■ Pitlochry

Known for its idyllic river gorge, this little village was the site of a famous Jacobite victory at the Battle of Killiecrankie in 1689. Visit the Soldier's Leap, where a fleeing Redcoat soldier is said to have jumped the 5-m (18-ft) gorge to escape the Jacobites.

⑩ Montrose Basin Wildlife Centre

MAP E6 ■ (01674) 676 336 ■ Visitor Centre: open Mar–Oct: 10:30am–5pm daily (Nov–Feb: to 4pm Fri–Mon) ■ Adm ■ www.scottish wildlifetrust.org.uk

Montrose is a tidal basin mecca for seafowl and waders. In winter, up to 80,000 pink-footed geese stop here during their migration.

Forth Rail Bridge from Queensferry Harbour

Places to Eat and Drink

PRICE CATEGORIES

For a three-course meal for one with half a bottle of wine (or equivalent meal), taxes and extra charges.

£ under £30   ££ £30–60   £££ over £60

1 Glen Clova Hotel
MAP E5 ■ Glen Clova, nr Kirriemuir ■ (01575) 550 350 ■ ££

Sitting at the end of a lovely glen, this hotel and restaurant has a simple all-day menu of staples including haddock, venison and steaks, as well as vegetarian options such as veggie haggis burgers.

2 Old Course Hotel
MAP F5 ■ St Andrews ■ (01334) 474 371 ■ £££

For lovers of fine dining, the hotel's Road Hole Restaurant offers French-influenced cuisine, while the menu at Sands is more cosmopolitan, journeying from North Africa to Italy.

3 63 Tay Street
MAP E5 ■ 63 Tay St, Perth ■ (01738) 441 451 ■ Closed D Sun & Mon ■ ££

This restaurant is the talk of the town, owing to chef Graeme Pallister. An extensive wine list complements a thrilling menu, which makes full use of Perthshire's prime natural larder.

4 Pillars of Hercules
MAP F5 ■ Strathmiglo Rd, Falkland ■ (01337) 857 749 ■ £

A family-friendly café, this place offers delicious vegetarian soups, sandwiches as well as main meals.

5 The Cellar
MAP F5 ■ Anstruther, Fife ■ (01333) 310 378 ■ Closed Sun–Tue ■ £££

A seafood heaven, this restaurant (see p64) is set off a courtyard behind the Fisheries Museum. Enjoy meat dishes, and some of the best fish in Scotland. Some dishes feature garlic shoots and sea buckthorn.

Welcoming entrance of The Peat Inn

6 The Peat Inn
MAP F5 ■ Cupar ■ (01334) 840 206 ■ Closed Sun & Mon ■ £££

Experience exceptional food and range of wine at the fairest prices, at this popular restaurant (see p64).

7 Andrew Fairlie
MAP F4 ■ Gleneagles Hotel ■ (01764) 694 267 ■ Closed Sun ■ £££

Head to Scotland's sole two-Michelin starred restaurant for terrific food.

8 Jute Café Bar
MAP E5 ■ Dundee Contemporary Arts Centre, 152 Nethergate, Dundee ■ (01382) 909 246 ■ ££

The cavernous interior at the Jute Café Bar is ultrahip. There is a range of beers available and the menu offers imaginative dishes at extremely reasonable prices.

9 Ship Inn
MAP F5 ■ Elie, Fife ■ (01333) 330 246 ■ ££

Seasonal food is served in a converted boathouse overlooking the harbour of this village. There is a bar below, and a bistro on top. Vegetarian options are available.

10 The But 'n' Ben
MAP E6 ■ Auchmithie, nr Arbroath ■ (01241) 877 223 ■ ££

Within the white walls of this old fisherman's cottage, seafood is the speciality, especially Arbroath Smokies (see p65). You'll also find good venison and local produce here.

See map on p90

Glasgow

Down-to-earth Glasgow has a dynamic and friendly character, something exemplified by its outgoing locals. From the highs and lows of its storied past, the city of Glasgow has endured. Today it has reinvented itself as something of an epicentre of culture, cuisine, shopping and entertainment. Magnificent buildings are scattered across the city alongside first-rate restaurants, while the patronage of wealthy collectors has ensured the exceptional quality of Glasgow's many museums, art galleries and gardens.

Stained-glass window, Glasgow Cathedral

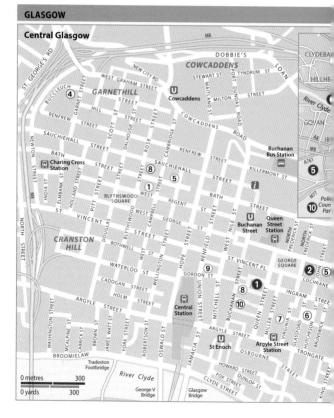

GLASGOW

① Gallery of Modern Art

MAP X4 ■ Royal Exchange Square ■ (0141) 287 3050 ■ Open 10am–5pm daily (from 11am Fri–Sun; to 8pm Thu)

Glasgow's Gallery of Modern Art includes some works that immediately grab your attention, others that are deviously clever and a few that are outrageously funny, but the ethos remains essentially the same. Its four main galleries showcase contemporary art and offer a consistently lively and thought-provoking programme of workshops and temporary exhibitions, featuring brilliant work by Scottish and international artists. In the basement is a sofa-adorned library with a café.

Lavish interior of City Chambers

② City Chambers

MAP Y4 ■ George Square ■ (0141) 287 4018 ■ By official tour only: 10:30am & 2:30pm Mon–Fri ■ www.glasgow.gov.uk

"Palace" would be a more appropriate term, for this is the finest seat of any council in Britain. Modelled on Classical Italian architecture, the building was designed by William Young and completed in 1889. The exterior is dramatic enough, but the interior is an exercise in the excesses of lavish decor. Aberdeen granite, Carrara marble, mahogany, gold leaf, frescoes, mosaics, pillars and balustrades are combined to astonishing effect. The Banqueting Hall – with its murals, chandeliers and ornately patterned ceiling and carpet – does not fail to impress.

③ Glasgow Cathedral and Necropolis

MAP Z3 ■ Cathedral Square ■ (0141) 552 6891 ■ Open Apr–Sep: 9:30am–5pm Mon–Sat, 1–4:30pm Sun; Oct–Mar: 10am–3:30pm Mon–Sat, 1–3:30pm Sun

Immense and ancient, this cathedral was ranked by Pope Nicholas V in 1451 as equal in merit to Rome as a place of pilgrimage. Dedicated in 1136 and completed almost a century later, it has been in continuous use since then and has the original roof timbers. The choir screen is unique in Scotland, and the postwar stained-glass windows are exceptional. On a hill to the east looms the Necropolis, a Victorian cemetery crowned by a monument to John Knox (see p14).

Top 10 Sights
see pp97–9

Places to Eat and Drink
see p101

The Best of the Rest
see p100

4 Kelvingrove Art Gallery and Museum

This world-famous museum is home to 22 fascinating galleries, whose exhibits span more than 5,000 years of human art and ingenuity, from Ancient Egypt to the 21st century (see pp20–21).

Stained glass, House for an Art Lover

5 House for an Art Lover

MAP Y3 ■ Bellahouston Park, Dumbreck Rd ■ (0141) 483 1600 ■ Open 10am–12:30pm Sat & Sun, 10am–4pm Mon–Fri (often closed for functions) ■ Adm ■ www.houseforan artlover.co.uk

In 1901 Glasgow's tour-de-force architect, Charles Rennie Mackintosh, and his artist wife, Margaret Macdonald, entered a magazine competition to design a "House for an Art Lover". It was to be "a grand house, thoroughly modern, fresh and innovative". Their exquisite vision remained just a design until 1989, when, precise to the smallest detail, the building and its contents were created. The café and shop are superb.

6 Riverside Museum

With acres of gleaming metalwork this museum (see pp22–3) has hundreds and hundreds of every-thing on wheels, including bicycles, cars, lorries, buses, trains and fire engines. You can walk through or climb into the larger vehicles, or sit in an original Glasgow tram. Highlights include a series of recreated early 20th-century Glasgow streets, and over 200 model ships illustrating the history of Clyde shipbuilding. Make sure you also visit the Tall Ship, moored outside. Built in the 19th century, it has sailed around the world four times.

7 People's Palace

MAP Z3 ■ Glasgow Green ■ (0141) 276 0788 ■ Open 10am–5pm Tue–Sun (from 11am Fri & Sun) ■ www.glasgowlife.org.uk/museums

Typically Glaswegian, this is a museum of ordinary life. Nothing fancy or outstandingly old, but a fascinating insight into how the average family lived, worked and played in the not-so-distant past. There are prints, photos and films as well as an array of objects.

8 Glasgow Science Centre

Myriad puzzles, experiments and demonstrations (see p61) to entertain and inform. There's also an IMAX screen and a revolving tower – a sensational place.

Exterior of Glasgow Science Centre

Kibble Palace, Botanic Gardens

⑨ Botanic Gardens

MAP Z2 ■ 730 Great Western Rd, Glasgow ■ (0141) 276 1614 ■ Gardens: open 7am–dusk daily ■ Glasshouses: open 10am–6pm daily (winter: to 4:15pm)

The highlights are the glasshouses famous for their tropicana (see p49).

⑩ Burrell Collection and Pollok Park

MAP Y3 ■ Pollokshaws Rd ■ (0141) 616 6410 ■ House: open 10am–5pm ■ Adm (free for NTS members) ■ www.nts.org.uk

Sir William Burrell's (1861–1958) superb collection, housed in a purpose-designed building, has long been one of Glasgow's finest attractions. Highlights include beautifully crafted stained glass and Degas' evocative painting *The Red Ballet Skirts*. The nearby Pollok House gives a fascinating insight into Edwardian life and has Spanish paintings by Murillo, El Greco and Goya. There's a café in the original kitchen, and lovely walks in the surrounding parkland.

ST MUNGO

A priest called St Mungo laid the foundations of Glasgow when he set up a monastery here in the 6th century. A settlement grew up around the monastery and prospered long after the demise of that early religious community. St Mungo's body lies beneath the cathedral, and his name has been given to a museum (see p100) of religious art.

A FULL DAY IN GLASGOW

▶ MORNING

Take the subway to Kelvinhall station (or walk from the city centre) to visit **Kelvingrove Art Gallery and Museum**. Allow a couple of hours to explore and don't miss the Dutch Old Masters and French Impressionists.

Walk to the **Hunterian Art Gallery** (see p100), on the other side of Kelvingrove Park, to explore the stunning **House for an Art Lover**, a reassemblage of the interiors of Charles Rennie Mackintosh's home. Tours start at 10am (11am on Sunday). Lunch at one of the many cafés on the nearby Byres Road or walk on to reach the **Botanic Gardens**, where you can picnic in the grounds or enjoy a meal in their tearoom. Stroll through the gardens and admire the orchids in the enormous, tropical Kibble Palace glasshouse.

AFTERNOON

Take the subway to Cowcaddens station, from where it's a short walk to the **Tenement House** (see p100). This intriguing, gas-lit property is laid out much as it was when it was home to Agnes Toward in the early 20th century; it's a real slice of old Glasgow life.

Hop back on the subway to Buchanan Street station, where you can choose to walk down to elegant **Princes Square** (see p100) to browse the shops window displays, or make your way across George Square in time for the 2:30pm tour of the **City Chambers** (see p97). Have dinner at one of the city's many fine restaurants.

The Best of the Rest

1 St Mungo Museum of Religious Art

MAP Z3 ■ 2 Castle St ■ (0141) 276 1625

Excellent overview of the world's religions through their art. The museum is illuminated by beautiful stained-glass windows.

2 Waverley Excursions

MAP Z3 ■ Anderston Quay ■ (0141) 243 2224 ■ Open Jun–Aug ■ www.waverleyexcursions.co.uk

Travel back in time and experience the Firth of Clyde on the world's last seagoing paddle steamer.

3 Hunterian Art Gallery

MAP Z2 ■ 82 Hillhead St, nr Kelvingrove Park ■ Open 10am–5pm Tue–Sun ■ www.gla.ac.uk/hunterian

This gallery is best known for its collection of Rembrandts, its works by 19th-century American artist Whistler and the Mackintosh House.

4 Tenement House

MAP W2 ■ 145 Buccleuch St ■ (0141) 333 0183 ■ Open Jan–Feb: 10am–5pm Fri–Sun; Mar–Dec: 10am–5pm Thu–Mon ■ Adm ■ www.nts.org

Tenements were standard Glasgow flats and Agnes Toward lived an ordinary life in this one, now a museum, for over 50 years.

5 The Wonderwall

MAP Y4 ■ 50 George St ■ Open 24 hrs daily ■ www.city centremuraltrail.co.uk)

The huge mural highlights the achievements of the innovators and technologists of the University of Strathclyde.

6 Merchant City

MAP Y4

East of George Square is this grid-plan of streets where the "Tobacco Lords" built their warehouses and mansions. The area is now full of designer shops and restaurants.

7 Provand's Lordship

MAP Z3 ■ 3 Castle St ■ (0141) 276 1625 ■ Open 10am–5pm Tue–Thu & Sat (from 11am Fri & Sun)

Built in 1471, this is the oldest house in Glasgow, with a fine furniture collection and cloistered herb garden.

8 Mackintosh at the Willow

MAP X3 ■ 215-217 Sauchiehall St ■ (0141) 204 1903 ■ www.mackintosh atthewillow.com

Credited to renowned Glasgow designer Charles Rennie Mackintosh in 1903, this tearoom is also an exhibition centre.

9 Citizens Theatre

MAP Z3 ■ 119 Gorbals St ■ (0141) 429 0022 ■ www.citz.co.uk

An internationally famous venue; two modern studios complement the old Victorian auditorium.

10 Princes Square

MAP X4 ■ 48 Buchanan St ■ (0141) 221 0324

Luxurious shopping centre in a renovated square of 1841 – the genteel atmosphere found here is heightened by the occasional appearance of a piano player.

Princes Square shopping centre

Places to Eat and Drink

PRICE CATEGORIES

For a three-course meal for one with half a bottle of wine (or equivalent meal), taxes and extra charges.

£ under £30   ££ £30–60   £££ over £60

1 Brian Maule at Chardon D'Or

MAP X3 ▪ 176 West Regent St ▪ (0141) 248 3801 ▪ Closed Sun & Mon ▪ £££

A true fine-dining experience that should not be missed *(see p64)*. The chef, Brian Maule, combines the greatness of classic French cuisine with modern dishes that use top-quality Scottish produce.

2 Ubiquitous Chip

MAP Y2 ▪ 12 Ashton Lane, off Byres Rd, Hillhead ▪ (0141) 334 5007 ▪ ££

Operating on this cobbled West End road since 1971, and always a champion of Scottish produce, the Ubiquitous Chip restaurant is Glasgow at its most endearing.

3 Stravaigin

MAP Z2 ▪ 28 Gibson St, Hillhead ▪ (0141) 334 2665 ▪ ££

Where the nation's fish, beef, lamb and game are mixed with the world's sauces, herbs and spices. Eclectic mix of flavours, but Stravaigin's judicious touch wins the day.

4 Gloriosa

MAP Y2 ▪ 1321 Argyle St, nr Kelvingrove Museum ▪ (0141) 334 0594 ▪ ££

Popular for its Mediterranean-inspired menu this hangout also has wood fired pizzas that are consistently excellent.

5 Sarti

MAP X3 ▪ 121 Bath St & 133 Wellington St & 42 Renfield St ▪ (0141) 572 7000 ▪ ££

Lively Italian displaying a love of food in a living, breathing, everyday sense. Restaurant on Bath Street, with a café and deli around the corner.

6 Chinaski's

MAP Z2 ▪ 239 North St ▪ (0141) 221 0061 ▪ £

The soundtrack here is one of the best in Glasgow, combining blues, soul and reggae. There is a heated deck and the food is enticing.

Stylish interior of Cup Merchant City

7 Cup Merchant City

MAP Y4 ▪ 4 Virginia Court ▪ (0141) 553 2326 ▪ ££

This delightful tearoom has pleasant courtyard seating and offers a wide range of afternoon menus, including gluten free, vegetarian and vegan options.

8 Rogano

MAP X4 ▪ 11 Exchange Place, off Exchange Square ▪ (0141) 248 4055 ▪ ££

A wonderful place to imbibe splendid cocktails in Art Deco surrounds. Pricey in the restaurant but fresh seafood is a bargain in the brasserie.

9 The Horseshoe Bar

MAP X4 ▪ 17 Drury St ▪ (0141) 248 6368 ▪ £

Few pubs deserve to be considered a Glasgow institution more than this gem of a place. Friendly and cheap, it is a cracking pub in which to soak up the city's ambience.

10 Mother India

MAP Z2 ▪ 28 Westminster Terrace, Sauchiehall St ▪ (0141) 221 1663 ▪ ££

A must-visit destination for gourmands of all stripes. You'll find exquisite modern Indian food here.

See map on pp96–7

TOP 10 North and West of Glasgow

This bucolic region became the focus of Scotland's first tourist industry in early Victorian times and, with Loch Lomond and the Trossachs National Park at its splendid centre, that allure remains as strong today. In the west are the rocky peaks of the Isle of Arran and a seaboard of fjord-like lochs, where a mild climate supports some grand gardens. In the east stands Stirling – a key city in the country's warring past – its mighty clifftop castle overlooking lush farmland. Here, William Wallace and Robert the Bruce fought for independence, a battle eventually won within sight of the castle on the field of Bannockburn.

Wallace Monument

NORTH AND WEST OF GLASGOW

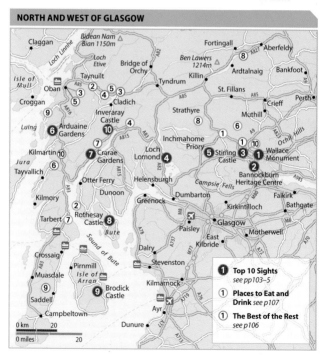

1 Top 10 Sights
see pp103–5

1 Places to Eat and
Drink see p107

1 The Best of the Rest
see p106

1 Wallace Monument

MAP F4 ▪ (01786) 472 140
▪ Open Apr–Jun, Sep & Oct: 9:30am–5pm daily (Jul & Aug: to 6pm); Nov–Mar: 10am–4pm daily ▪ Adm ▪ www. nationalwallacemonument.com

Erected in 1869, this 75-m (250-ft) tower commemorates William Wallace and his fight for Scotland's independence. The climb takes you past Wallace's two-handed broadsword, while a hologram-style display shows a disembodied "talking head" (meant to represent Wallace himself after decapitation) that recites his pre-execution defence speech.

2 Battle of Bannockburn Experience

MAP F4 ▪ Site: open all year
▪ Heritage Centre: open Feb–Dec: 10am–5pm daily; adm (free for NTS members); www.nts.org.uk

The site of the decisive battle (see p38) in 1314 is marked by a visitor centre and an equestrian statue of Robert the Bruce. Kids can try on helmets and chain mail, and view Bruce's cave to watch the fabled spider who inspired him to renew his fight.

Robert the Bruce, Bannockburn

3 Stirling Castle

MAP F4 ▪ (01786) 450 000
▪ Open Apr–Sep: 9:30am–6pm daily (Oct–Mar: to 5pm) ▪ Adm (free for HES members) ▪ www.stirlingcastle.scot

Perched on a massive rock, the Stirling Castle (see p40) conceals the unique architecture of the restored Great Hall and the Royal Palace.

Stirling Castle

The scenic Trossachs National Park

4 Loch Lomond and the Trossachs National Park

MAP F4 ▪ www.lochlomond-trossachs.org

The broad, friendly mountains and poetic scenery of Scotland's first national park are ideal for the casual walker and watersports lover. Luss is the prettiest village in the area, possessing a lovely sandy beach and some excellent restaurants. Cruises run from here, and from Balloch, Tarbet and Balmaha.

5 Inchmahome Priory

MAP F4 ▪ (01877) 385 294
▪ Closed for restoration ▪ Adm
▪ www.historicenvironment.scot

The Lake of Menteith is Scotland's only lake (as opposed to loch), and famed for the graceful ruined priory on the island of Inchmahome. It's in this beautiful spot that the infant Mary Queen of Scots was looked after by Augustinian monks before she was spirited away to France.

(6) Arduaine Gardens

MAP F3 ▪ Nr Oban ▪ (01852) 200 366 ▪ Closed for restoration ▪ Adm (free for NTS members) ▪ www.nts.org.uk

A dazzling assembly of rhododendrons, azaleas, magnolias and hosts of global species from the Pacific Islands to the Himalayas. Arduaine *(see p49)* is beautifully situated on a promontory between sea lochs, and glories in the warm winds from the Gulf Stream.

(7) Crarae Gardens

MAP F3 ▪ Nr Inveraray ▪ (01546) 886 614 ▪ Open Apr–Oct: 10am–5pm daily; Nov–Mar: 9:30am–4pm Thu–Mon; Visitor Centre: open Apr–Sep: 10am–4pm daily ▪ Adm (free for NTS members)

You don't have to be a rhododendron specialist to be bowled over by this beautifully manicured orchestration of colour *(see p49)*. An outstanding and rare collection, which is at its best in spring.

(8) Rothesay Castle, Bute

MAP F3 ▪ (01700) 502 691 ▪ Closed for restoration ▪ Adm (free for HES members)

By virtue of its age, design and deep-water moat (one of only two remaining in Scotland), this is a remarkable medieval castle. Built around 1200s as a defence against Norwegian raiders, it was restyled

Rothesay Castle, Bute

in the 13th century and fitted with high curtain walls and drum towers. Its circular courtyard is a curious feature and unique in Scotland. Bute itself is a mere 35-minute crossing from Wemyss Bay – north of Largs on the A78 – to Rothesay Bay; an even shorter crossing is from Colintraive to Rhubodach, on the north coast of the island.

(9) Brodick Castle, Arran

MAP G3 ▪ (01770) 302 202 ▪ Castle, Tearoom and Park: open Apr–Oct: 10:30am–5pm daily ▪ Adm (free for NTS members) ▪ www.nts.org.uk

Originally a Viking keep before the Dukes of Hamilton claimed it, this 13th-century fortified tower was extended by Oliver Cromwell and then transformed into a stately home in Victorian times. The last Hamilton moved out only in 1957. A solid red sandstone building with fanciful trimmings, it contains a noted collection of silver, porcelain and paintings. The gardens are beautifully maintained (try to catch the rhododendrons in spring bloom), as are the woodland trails. The main ferry to Arran (just under an hour) is from Ardrossan, on the mainland coast, just north of Irvine.

THE WONDERFUL WORLD OF CRARAE GARDENS

Lady Grace Campbell began to lay out the gardens in 1912, making exciting use of plant specimens that her nephew Reginald Farrer brought back from his travels to Tibet and the Himalayas. On the higher ground is the forest-garden, a feature that is found nowhere else in Britain, where more than 100 tree species grow under forest conditions on their own plots. Crarae is considered of international importance and is a member of "Glorious Gardens of Argyll and Bute" *(www.gardens-of-argyll.co.uk)*.

10 Inveraray Castle
MAP F3 ■ (01499) 302 203
■ Open Apr–Oct: 10am–5pm daily
■ Adm ■ www.inveraray-castle.com

Despite the ravages of fire, Clan Campbell's *(see p43)* family seat is a splendid pseudo-Gothic palace with pointed towers. It was built for the Duke of Argyll in 1745. The interiors were designed by Robert Mylne and contain Regency furniture and priceless works of art. The Armoury Hall was stocked to fight the Jacobites. There's a hilltop folly in the grounds. The castle grounds host the Inveraray Highland Games, a colourful celebration of Highland culture.

Armoury Hall, Inveraray Castle

A DAY IN THE TROSSACHS

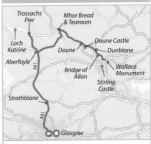

▶ MORNING

Reserve your morning cruise aboard the *Rob Roy III* or *Lady of the Lake* ([01877] 376 315, call in advance; www.lochkatrine.com).

Leaving **Glasgow** by 8:15am, drive north on the A81 to **Strathblane** and **Aberfoyle**. You are now in the scenic **Trossachs** *(see p103)*. Park at the **Trossachs Pier** for a 10:30am cruise on **Loch Katrine** *(see p44)*, a gorgeous loch.

Arriving back at 12:30pm, a short drive takes you to Kilmahog (great name, but the Woollen Mill is worth a visit if you're curious about knitwear). Head on to Callander, where you can stop for lunch at one of several restaurants, or buy delicious pies at the **Mhor Bread & Tearoom** *(Map F4; 8 Main St, Callander; [01877] 339 518; closed D)* and picnic by the river.

AFTERNOON

Carry on to **Doune**, **Dunblane** and **Bridge of Allan**. There are many temptations en route, including the **Doune Castle** *(see p106)*, a cathedral and a motor museum.

If not, head to **Wallace Monument** *(see p103)* before 4pm, and earlier in winter. Enjoy the history and the panoramic views of the area, including the craggy heights of **Stirling Castle** *(see p103)*.

Head back to Glasgow for an early dinner in the city centre *(see p101)*. For those who can wait, Edinburgh or St Andrews *(see p92)* are only slightly further towards the east (each about an hour's drive).

See map on p102

The Best of the Rest

① Doune Castle
MAP F4 ■ (01786) 841 742
■ Closed for restoration ■ Adm

The highlight of this 14th-century castle is the enchanting Lord's Hall, with its musicians' gallery and double fireplace.

The majestic Doune Castle

② Bonawe Historic Iron Furnace
MAP E3 ■ Taynuilt ■ (01866) 822 432
■ Open Apr–Sep: 9:30am–5:30pm daily ■ Adm (free for HES members) ■ www.historicenvironment.scot

Set by Loch Etive are these superbly preserved charcoal-fuelled ironworks, last operational in 1876.

③ St Conan's Kirk
MAP E3 ■ Lochawe village
■ Open Apr–Sep: 8am–6pm daily; Oct–Mar: 9am–5pm daily ■ Adm: donation suggested ■ www.stconans kirk.org.uk

With an eclectic architectural style, this remarkable church has three chapels, one of which contains a marble effigy of Robert the Bruce.

④ Cruachan Hollow Mountain Power Station
MAP E3 ■ Nr Lochawe ■ (0141) 614 9105 ■ Times vary, check website ■ Adm ■ www.visitcruachan.co.uk

Tunnels and underground caverns make this massive hydroelectric plant seem like a science-fiction set.

⑤ Oban
MAP E3 ■ Visitor Info: (01631) 563 122

This busy harbour town is best seen from McCaig's Folly. There are many local attractions here and ferries travelling to Mull, Coll, Colonsay, Tiree and the Western Isles.

⑥ Crinan Canal
MAP F3

Take a stroll along this scenic 16-km (9-mile) canal, completed in 1801, and now used by yachts and fishing boats. The best places to see them are at Ardrishaig, Cairnbaan or Crinan.

⑦ Auchindrain Township
MAP F3 ■ Nr Inveraray
■ (01499) 500 235 ■ Closed for restoration ■ Adm ■ www. auchindrain.org.uk

A novel outdoor museum of restored thatched cottages and outbuildings, Auchindrain displays the past styles of West Highland life.

⑧ Scottish Crannog Centre
MAP E4 ■ Kenmore ■ (01887) 830 583 ■ Open Apr–Oct: 10am–5:30pm daily ■ Adm ■ www.crannog.co.uk

The little-known and ancient art of building *crannogs* (defensive home-steads built on stilts in lochs) is brought to life at the museum here.

⑨ Kintyre
MAP G3 ■ www. wildaboutargyll.co.uk

Paul McCartney sang about this glorious peninsula, which has miles of beaches, a top golf course (Machrihanish) and the ethereal cave crucifixion painting on Davaar Island.

⑩ Kilmartin Glen
MAP F3

Inhabited for 5,000 years, the area is dense with archaeological remains such as standing stones and temples. Pause at Kilmartin Church for their collection of early Christian crosses.

Places to Eat and Drink

PRICE CATEGORIES

For a three-course meal for one with half a bottle of wine (or equivalent meal), taxes and extra charges.

£ under £30   ££ £30–60   £££ over £60

① The Roman Camp
MAP F4 ■ Callander ■ (01877) 330 003 ■ £££

Voluptuous curtains, deep sofas and blazing fires make this country hotel a delight, and the restaurant excels. Their Sunday lunch special, rump of lamb, is a winner.

② Marina Restaurant
MAP F3 ■ Portavadie, Loch Fyne ■ (01700) 811 075 ■ ££

Loch Fyne oysters and fresh seafood are served in this lovely restaurant that offers splendid views of Kintyre and the distant Arran Hills.

③ Ee-Usk
MAP E3 ■ North Pier, Oban ■ (01631) 565 666 ■ ££

Fresh seafood straight from Oban harbour is served in a modern building with huge windows and sea views.

④ Loch Fyne Oyster Bar
MAP F3 ■ Cairndow, nr Inveraray ■ (01499) 600 482 ■ ££

Long established in this converted stone cattle byre, this brilliant oyster bar offers an ocean of the freshest seafood, including loin of cod, smoked haddock, lobster and, of course, oysters.

Loch Fyne Oyster Bar

⑤ The Drover's Inn
MAP F4 ■ Inverarnan, Loch Lomond ■ (01301) 704 234 ■ ££

A flagstone floor, cobwebbed walls and a menagerie of stuffed animals to fight your way past – it's quite an experience. Good ol' pub grub and amber fluid flow all day.

⑥ The Kailyard
MAP F4 ■ Perth Rd, Dunblane FK15 OHG ■ (01786) 822 551 ■ ££

Fine Scottish produce is served at this hotel restaurant, run by celebrity chef Nick Nairn. The dishes served include Scotch beef and Scrabster sole. It also has a good vegetarian menu.

⑦ Starfish
MAP F2 ■ Castle St, Tarbert ■ (01880) 820 733 ■ ££

Set in a picturesque fishing village, this friendly and relaxed restaurant with local art on the walls serves up langoustines, lobster, scallops, crab and other seafood – all of which is landed daily at the nearby quay.

⑧ The Waterfront
MAP E4 ■ Kenmore ■ (01877) 830 829 ■ ££

Overlooking Loch Tay, this sleek and modern restaurant serves dishes prepared with fresh local produce. Try the haddock, venison and sea trout. Vegetarian options are available.

⑨ Tigh-an-Truish
MAP F3 ■ Clachan, Isle of Seil ■ (01852) 300 242 ■ ££

Old-world inn by the famous "Bridge over the Atlantic"; you half expect pirates to breeze in. Real ale and delicious local food.

⑩ Hermann's
MAP F4 ■ 58 Broad St, Stirling ■ (01786) 450 632 ■ www.hermanns. co.uk ■ ££

A long-standing local favourite, famed for fine Scottish steaks and Austrian dishes such as schnitzel and *spätzle*.

See map on p102

TOP 10 Grampian and Moray

The northeastern corner of Scotland, a veritable medley of landscapes, is home to equally diverse industries, from the traditions of farming, fishing and distilling to the more recent business of North Sea oil extraction. The high granite massif of the Cairngorms is primed for mountain sports. Then comes the forested splendour of Royal Deeside, Queen Victoria's beloved retreat, and the quilted fields of Buchan's rich farmland. Along the River Spey is the heartland of whisky production, while on the coast are beaches, cliffs and enchanting fishing villages.

Bishop Elphinstones tomb at Old Aberdeen

1 Aberdeen

MAP D6 ■ Aberdeen Science Centre: 179 Constitution St; (01224) 640 340 ■ Provost Skene's House, Guestrow: (0300) 020 0293 ■ Maritime Museum, Shiprow: (01224) 337 700 ■ Art Gallery, Schoolhill: (03000) 200 293

The "Granite City" has beautiful buildings, year-round floral displays and a beach fringed with entertainment, including the Beach Leisure Centre (see p61) and the Aberdeen Science Centre, a science discovery complex. Provost Skene's House (once home to a 17th-century *provost*, or mayor, of Aberdeen) is the oldest building, dating from 1545, while Marischal College is one of the world's largest granite edifices. The Maritime Museum charts the nautical world from shipbuilding to shipwrecks, while the Art Gallery combines temporary contemporary shows with a permanent collection spanning the 19th–20th centuries.

GRAMPIAN AND MORAY

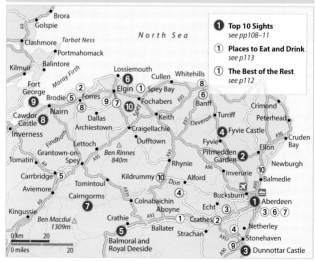

Top 10 Sights
see pp108–11

Places to Eat and Drink
see p113

The Best of the Rest
see p112

The meticulously landscaped Great Garden, Pitmedden Garden

② Pitmedden Garden
MAP D6 ■ Ellon ■ (01651) 842 352 ■ Grounds: daily ■ Garden, museum & shop: open Apr–late Sep: 10:30am–4:30pm daily (Oct: Fri–Mon) ■ Adm (free for NTS members)

The striking symmetry of the formal Great Garden *(see p49)* is unique. The wildlife gardens and the Museum of Farming Life are hits, too.

③ Dunnottar Castle
MAP E6 ■ Nr Stonehaven ■ (01569) 766 320 ■ Times vary, check website (may be closed during bad weather) ■ Adm ■ www.dunnottar castle.co.uk

Standing strikingly on a rock, few castles match Dunnottar's setting or have endured such intense bombardments. In 1651, while harbouring the Scottish royalty who were secretly smuggled out by a brave woman, it withstood an eight-month siege by the English. Some 800 years of attack have taken their toll, but Dunnottar remains a mythical sight.

④ Fyvie Castle
MAP D6 ■ Nr Turriff ■ (01651) 891 266 ■ Castle: open Apr–Dec: 10:30am–4:30pm Thu–Sun; guided tours only ■ Garden: 9am–sunset daily ■ Adm ■ www.nts.org.uk

Dating from 1390, this formidable building, which once hosted Charles I, is one of the finest examples of Scottish Baronial architecture. Its life through the ages is testified to by the mix of contemporary panelling, 17th-century plasterwork and treasure trove of collectable paintings, arms and armour. The restored 19th-century Victorian walled garden specializes in Scottish fruit and vegetables.

Fyvie Castle

Balmoral Castle, the Queen's summer residence in Royal Deeside

(5) Balmoral and Royal Deeside

MAP D5 ■ (01339) 742 534 ■ Open Apr–Jul: 10am–5pm daily; Oct–Dec: times vary, check website ■ Adm ■ www.balmoralcastle.com

Queen Victoria bought this castle in 1852. Balmoral, bordering the salmon pools of the River Dee, remains the holiday home of the monarch to this day and, consequently, the rolling countryside around the banks of the river has taken on the royal moniker. Cast an eye round the castle's sumptuous ballroom, then make the most of the enchanting forest walks.

(6) Moray Coast Villages

MAP C5–6

These charming communities thrived in the herring boom of the 19th century, but today only Lossiemouth, Buckie (with its excellent Drifter Museum), Macduff and Fraserburgh continue as fishing ports. For many visitors, Crovie (pronounced "crivie") is the pick of the bunch. Access from the car park is by foot only, its picturesque street strung out below the cliffs – it truly is a fabulous setting. The walk to Gardenstown is an adventure for the sure-footed. Findhorn – famous for its spiritual community – is beautifully located on a sandy lagoon. A self-drive tour of the coastal road (highly recommended) will reveal a dozen other villages, each one possessing its own unique character.

Crovie village, Moray Coast

VICTORIA AND ALBERT'S BALMORAL

It was the riverside setting that Victoria fell for in 1848 when she first visited Balmoral. And it was her husband Albert who worked with the Aberdeen-born architect William Smith to create the white granite palace that replaced the old castle and stands here still, a medley of fantastical turrets typical of the Baronial style.

7 Cairngorms

A superb range of mountain peaks *(see pp34–5)* surrounded by pine forests and lochs. Ideal for testing walks, lively watersports and inspiring scenery.

8 Cawdor Castle

MAP D4 ■ Nr Nairn ■ (01667) 404 401 ■ Open May–early Oct: 10am–5:30pm daily ■ Adm ■ www.cawdor castle.com

A private home, handed down through the generations since the time when Macbeth lived here (or so legend has it). Cawdor Castle *(see p41)* is full of history and delight, with creepy relics, magnificent trees and a garden maze.

9 Fort George

MAP D4

On a peninsula jutting into the Moray Firth is this vast fort complex *(see p29)*, built at enormous expense 250 years ago and still used as an army barracks today. Impressive defences now guard a vintage armoury. Check out the special summer events.

10 The Whisky Trail

Seven of Scotland's finest malt whisky distilleries *(see p35)* invite you inside. Apart from the magic of the shining copper stills, the once-secretive process of whisky-making is revealed, enthusiasm infused and the precious *uisge beatha* (water of life) consumed.

A DAY'S DRIVING TOUR

▶ MORNING

Leave **Aberdeen** *(see p108)* around 9am and drive on the A93 through Deeside's splendid scenery to Crathie, where you'll find the castle in **Balmoral** opening its gates. If, however, you're outside Balmoral's short opening season, then visit **Crathes Castle** or **Drum Castle** *(see p112)* instead – less famous, but equally impressive.

Return to Ballater, the nearest town to Balmoral Castle which you passed through on the way, but this time take the B976 on the south of the river. There are plenty of places to eat, offering anything from a bacon sandwich or pain au chocolat to a three-course meal.

AFTERNOON

While browsing the shops in Ballater, look out for royal insignias: they indicate the Queen's favourite establishments.

From Ballater find the A939 and drive north on a twisting road. The terrain is wild, heathery moorland and mountainous. The road takes you past quaint and lonely Corgarff Castle, and on to Tomintoul, one of the highest villages in Scotland. From here, take the B9008 to the distillery of **Glenlivet** *(see p60)* for a tour of their whisky-making vats, stills and barrels, and a tasting. Tours last about 75 minutes; the tastings, unfortunately, much less.

Spend the night around Dufftown or Keith and plan to drive to Portsoy on the coast road either east or west the next day. The tour is about 150 km (90 miles) in total.

See map on p108

The Best of the Rest

① Moray Firth Dolphins
MAP D4 ■ Boat trips from Inverness: (07544) 800 620, www.dolphinspirit.co.uk ■ Boat trips from Nairn, Findhorn and Lossiemouth: (0130) 969 099; www.north58.co.uk

The only known resident population of bottlenose dolphins in the North Sea. The best place to see them from land is Chanonry Point on the Black Isle.

② Crathes Castle
MAP D6 ■ Banchory ■ (01330) 844 525 ■ Castle: Times vary, call ahead ■ Grounds: open all year ■ Adm (free for NTS members)

A 16th-century tower house, with a traditional Great Hall. There are topiary and plant sales Easter to October.

③ Drum Castle
MAP D6 ■ Nr Banchory ■ (01330) 700 334 ■ Castle: Times vary, call ahead ■ Grounds: open all year ■ Adm (free for NTS members)

This is one of the three oldest surviving tower houses in Scotland.

④ Craigievar Castle
MAP D6 ■ (01339) 883635 ■ Castle: open Apr & May: 10:30am–4pm Fri–Tue (Jun–Sep: daily; Oct: to 3pm Sat & Sun) ■ Grounds: open all year ■ Adm (free for NTS members)

A tower house with porcelain details. There are monkey puzzle trees here.

The striking Craigievar Castle

⑤ Brodie Castle
MAP D4 ■ Forres, nr Nairn ■ (01309) 641 ■ Castle: Times vary, call ahead ■ Grounds: open all year ■ Adm (free for NTS members)

This Z-Plan tower house has survived many attacks and contains a treasury of furniture and paintings.

⑥ Duff House Gallery
MAP C6 ■ Banff ■ (01261) 818 181 ■ Open Apr–Sep: 9:30am–1pm & 2–5pm Thu–Sun; Oct–Mar: 10am–4pm Fri–Sun ■ Adm (free for HES members) ■ www.historicenvironment.scot

The collection at this Georgian mansion includes works by Ramsay and Raeburn, as well as El Greco.

⑦ Elgin Cathedral
MAP C5 ■ (01343) 547 171 ■ Open Apr–Sep: 9:30am–5:30pm daily; Oct–Mar: 10am–4pm daily ■ Adm (free for HES members)

Burned out of spite by the Wolf of Badenoch in 1390, this cathedral's picturesque ruins draw a crowd.

⑧ Dallas Dhu Distillery
MAP C5 ■ Forres, nr Nairn ■ (01309) 676548 ■ Open Apr–Sep: 9:30am–5:30pm Mon–Sat; Oct–Mar: 10am–4pm Sat–Wed ■ Adm (free for HES members)

When this working distillery closed, it was preserved as a time capsule of whisky-making from 1898 to 1980.

⑨ Stonehaven
MAP E6

Close to Dunnottar Castle *(see p109)*, this seaside resort has a heated open-air Olympic-size swimming pool.

⑩ Kildrummy Castle
MAP D5 ■ Nr Alford ■ (01975) 571 1331 ■ Open Apr–Sep: 9:30am–5:30pm Sun–Mon ■ Adm (free for HES members)

The once "noblest of northern castles" is now a grandiose ruin but retains many unique 13th-century features.

Places to Eat and Drink

At the Sign of the Black Faced Sheep

PRICE CATEGORIES

For a three-course meal for one with half a bottle of wine (or equivalent meal), taxes and extra charges.

£ under £30 ■ ££ £30–60 ■ £££ over £60

1 At the Sign of the Black Faced Sheep

MAP D5 ■ Ballater Rd, Aboyne
■ (01339) 887 311 ■ £

Emporium with an upmarket coffee shop serving interesting sandwiches, sun-dried tomato scones, seafood platters, daily specials and great cakes.

2 The Bakehouse Cafe

MAP C5 ■ 91-92 Findhorn Rd, Forres
■ (01309) 691826 ■ £

This is a great place for vegetarian dishes and organic produce. It does some delicious home baking as well.

3 210 Bistro

MAP D6 ■ 210 South Market St, Aberdeen ■ (01224) 211857
■ Closed Sun ■ ££

The downstairs café and bar forms a relaxing anteroom between bustling Market Street and the upstairs restaurant with its minimalist decor, and harbour views. The menu features fresh and beautifully presented Scottish dishes.

4 Tolbooth Restaurant

MAP E6 ■ Stonehaven
■ (01569) 762 287 ■ ££

With fabulous harbour views, this sparkling little restaurant in Stonehaven's oldest building is a great spot to treat yourself with inventive seafood dishes such as curry dusted monkfish.

5 Anderson's

MAP D4 ■ Boat of Garten
■ (01479) 831 466 ■ ££

Classy little restaurant offering a short, excellent menu that combines Scottish and European cuisines beautifully.

6 The Silver Darling

MAP D6 ■ Pocra Quay, Aberdeen ■ (01224) 576 229 ■ ££

One of the best restaurants in the country, this seafood emporium (see p65) overlooks the Aberdeen harbour.

7 Moonfish Café

MAP D6 ■ 9 Correction Wynd, Aberdeen ■ (01224) 644 166 ■ ££

Tucked away in a lane, this place is known for some of Aberdeen's most inventive fare.

A dish at Moonfish Café

8 The Seafield Arms

MAP D5–6 ■ 5 Chapel St, Whitehills, nr Banff
■ (01261) 861 209 ■ ££

Set on the Moray Firth, this inn focuses on seafood dishes. Try the baked haddock with tiger prawns.

9 The Sunninghill Hotel

MAP C5 ■ Hay St, Elgin
■ (01343) 547 799 ■ ££

Popular with locals, this hotel serves traditional Scottish dishes such as steak pie and fresh haddock with chips.

10 Cock and Bull

MAP D6 ■ Ellon Rd, Balmedie
■ (01358) 743 249 ■ ££

Rustic meets trendy in this blend of country inn and contemporary gastropub. Try the fish cakes or a juicy burger.

See map on p108

TOP 10 The Highlands

The name alone evokes thoughts of mountains, heather, bagpipes, castles, clans, romance and tragedy – indeed, the Highlands have it all. It is the combination of peerless scenery, enduring traditions and nostalgia (albeit for a rather idealized past) that gives the Highlands their irresistible allure. It's a sparsely inhabited region, where you may still find plenty of single-track roads and a lot more sheep than people. Life takes on a slower pace here, and often hotels and restaurants work shorter hours, but the great compensation is peace. Little wonder that so many aspects of the Highlands have been adopted as symbols of the nation as a whole.

Memorial Cairn, Culloden Battlefield

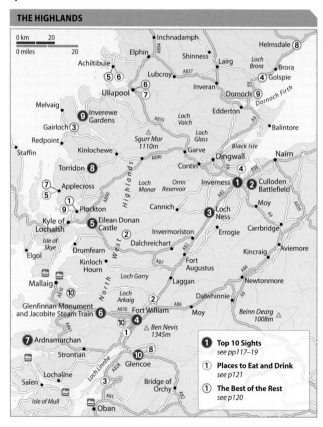

THE HIGHLANDS

0 km 20
0 miles 20

Inchnadamph
Elphin
Achiltibuie
Shinness
Lairg
Helmsdale 8
Loch Brora
Brora
⑤ ⑥ Lubcroy A837
Inveran
Golspie ④
⑥ Ullapool
⑦
Dornoch ⑨
Dornoch Firth
Melvaig
⑨ Inverewe Gardens
Edderton
Loch Vaich
Gairloch ③
A835
Redpoint
Loch Glass
Balintore
Staffin
Kinlochewe
Sgurr Mor 1110m
Garve
Black Isle
Torridon ⑧
Contin
Dingwall
Nairn
⑦ Applecross
Highlands
Loch Monar
Orrin Reservoir
Inverness ① ②
Culloden Battlefield
⑤
① Plockton
Cannich
④
Moy
⑨
Loch Ness ③
Kyle of Lochalsh
⑤ Eilean Donan Castle
Invermoriston
Errogie
Carrbridge
Isle of Skye
② Dalchreichart
Kincraig
Aviemore
Elgol
Drumfearn
Fort Augustus
North West Highlands
Kinloch Hourn
Loch Garry
Laggan
Newtonmore
Mallaig
⑩
Loch Arkaig
② Dalwhinnie
Glenfinnan Monument and Jacobite Steam Train ⑥
A830 Fort William
Moy
Beinn Dearg 1008m
⑩ ④
① △ Ben Nevis 1345m
⑦ Ardnamurchan
Strontian
⑩ ⑧ Glencoe
Lochaline
Loch Linnhe
③ Bridge of Orchy
Salen
Isle of Mull
A85
Oban

① **Top 10 Sights**
see pp117–19

① **Places to Eat and Drink**
see p121

① **The Best of the Rest**
see p120

The imposing Inverness castle

a peculiarly emotional experience. The Memorial Cairn, which was erected here in 1881, stands 6 m (20 ft) high. The story is well illustrated in the visitor centre.

3 Loch Ness

Ice Age glaciers gouged out a deep trench along a split in the land mass of Scotland, and the resulting valley is known as the Great Glen. Loch Ness (see pp28–9) is its main attraction, with arresting views, the mystery of its reclusive monster and the evocative ruins of Urquhart Castle.

1 Inverness

MAP D4 ▪ Tourist Info: (01463) 252 401 ▪ Museum & Gallery: Castle Hill; open Apr–Oct: 10am–5pm Tue–Sat; Nov–Mar: noon–4pm Tue–Thu, 11am–4pm Fri & Sat; adm ▪ Viewpoint: closed for restoration; adm ▪ Abertarff House: open 11am–6pm daily in summer, shorter hours in winter

A fast-growing city with a small-town feel, Inverness is home to a majestic red sandstone castle. Visit the Inverness Museum and Art Gallery, which provides an interesting insight into Highland heritage, as well as excellent temporary exhibitions. There's also the 1593 Abertarff House, the oldest house in Inverness, and the sublimely peaceful Ness Islands Walk.

2 Culloden Battlefield

MAP D4 ▪ Visitor Centre: (01463) 796 090; open Nov–Feb: 10am–4pm daily; Mar–May, Sep & Oct: 9am–6pm daily (Jun–Aug: to 7pm) ▪ Adm (free for NTS members) ▪ www.nts.org.uk

The last battle on British soil, 16th April 1746, was a defeat for Bonnie Prince Charlie and the Jacobites (see p38). The slaughter by the "Bloody Butcher's" (the Duke of Cumberland's) Hanoverian army was quick and brutal. The battlefield is gradually being restored to its appearance at the time of the bloodshed. To walk among the graves of the clans is still

4 Ben Nevis and Fort William

MAP E3 ▪ Tourist Info: (01397) 701 801 ▪ West Highland Museum: (01397) 702 169; open Jan–Apr & Oct–Dec: 10am–4pm Mon–Fri (May–Sep: to 4:30pm); Apr–Oct: 10:30am–1:30pm Sat ▪ Treasures of the Earth: (01397) 772 283; open daily

Britain's highest mountain (see p46) is 1,345 m (4,413 ft) high and offers a great walk in good conditions. But the peak is frequently shrouded in mist, and the drive up Glen Nevis offers a more reliable reward, taking you to a waterfall. Fort William (see p28) a major shopping town lies below the mountain, with plenty of attractions. Its West Highland Museum has many Jacobite relics, and Treasures of the Earth exhibits glittering heaps of gems.

Ben Nevis behind Fort William

5 Eilean Donan Castle
MAP D3 ▪ Visitor centre: (01599) 555 202 ▪ Open Feb–Dec: 10am–4pm daily (Apr–Sep: to 6pm) ▪ Adm ▪ www.eileandonancastle.com

Restored in 13th-century, this majestic fortress *(see p41)* of Clan Macrae stands on a picturesque island on the road to Skye.

6 Glenfinnan Monument and Jacobite Steam Train
MAP E3 ▪ Visitor centre: (01397) 722 250; open Apr–Nov: 10am–5pm daily (Dec–Mar: to 4pm); adm (free for NTS members ▪ Jacobite Steam Train: (0333) 996 6720; open May–Oct

This is another memorial to the Jacobite uprising led by Bonnie Prince Charlie *(see p38)*, on the site where his campaign began. Here, a visitor centre explains the history. The chief attraction is getting here – the scenery en route is stunning. Take time to marvel at the nearby viaduct (featured in the Harry Potter films) and wait for a passing steam train – or even better, be in a passing steam train.

Camas nan Geall, Ardnamurchan

Glenfinnan Monument

RETURN OF THE BONNIE PRINCE

Set on reclaiming the British Crown for the Stuart line, Bonnie Prince Charlie landed on the west coast of Scotland in 1745 with but a handful of men. His temerity, as well as widespread support for the Jacobite cause, won over many Scots, and when he came to raise his standard at Glenfinnan, numbers swelled as clans such as the Camerons rallied to his side.

7 Ardnamurchan
MAP E2 ▪ Natural History Centre: (01972) 500 209; open Mar–Oct: 9am–5pm Sun–Fri; www.ardnamurchan naturalhistorycentre.com

This peninsula – with its rugged mountains, pretty villages and what is one of the most delightful roads in the country, ending in a parade of white sand – is as lyrical in nature as it is in name. Acharacle is a famed den of musicians, while Glenmore is home to a Natural History Centre with a tearoom, gift shop and a "living building". Wild deer sometimes graze on its roof. From Kilchoan you can catch a ferry to Tobermory on Mull.

Torridon Hills, near Torridon village

8 Torridon
MAP D3 ■ Countryside Centre: (01445) 791 221; open Apr–Sep: 10am–5pm Sun–Fri ■ www.nts.org.uk

Flanked by a long sea loch, the red sandstone buttresses of Beinn Alligin, Ben Dearg, Liathach (the highest, see p47) and Beinn Eighe rise up into arresting outlines. From Little Diabaig you can walk a delightful coastal path to Alligin Shuas, or to Craig. The National Trust for Scotland runs an informative Countryside Centre with nearby herds of red deer and Highland cattle.

9 Inverewe Gardens
MAP C3 ■ Nr Poolewe
■ (01445) 712 952
■ Open Jan–late May & Sep: 9:45am–4pm daily (Jun–late Aug: to 5pm)

Butterfly, Inverewe Gardens

■ Adm (free for NTS members)

The sheer richness and variety of plant life growing here (see p49) in what many consider to be a cold wilderness is a tribute to a plant enthusiast's vision and hard work, nature's bounty and the surprising benign effects of warm Atlantic winds.

10 Glencoe
A rugged mountain range (see pp30–31) gathered into gorgeous scenery through which the twisting main road seems to creep submissively. A favourite skiing, mountaineering and walking area, and infamous for the terrible 1692 massacre of Clan MacDonald (see p30).

A HIGHLAND DAY TRIP

▶ MORNING

Pack a picnic in **Inverness** (see p117). There are lots of picnicking possibilities on this route, so make sure to take one.

Leave Inverness by 10am, taking the B852 to Dores and driving along the south side of **Loch Ness** (see p117) – a beautiful and much quieter road than that on the northern shore. Try to stop off at the **Falls of Foyers** (see p58).

Enjoy the hill-country drive to **Fort Augustus** (see p29), and pop in for a coffee at **The Lock Inn** (Map D4; Canal Side, PH32 4AU; (01320) 366 302), right beside the canal. Walk along the canal to view Loch Ness from the shore behind the old abbey.

Drive along the A82 on the north side of Loch Ness (stop at Invermoriston to view the river pools and old bridge) and visit **Urquhart Castle** (see p29). Have your picnic lunch here.

AFTERNOON

Having recharged your batteries sufficiently, visit one of the **Loch Ness Monster Visitor Centres** (see p29) in Drumnadrochit.

Refill your thermos in Drumnadrochit, then take the A831 to Cannich, and the minor road to **Glen Affric** (see p120).

Enjoy an hour's walk in this renowned beauty spot, before returning to the bustle of Inverness via Kilmorack and the south shore of the Beauly Firth. The entire round trip is about 185 km (115 miles).

See map on p116 ←

The Best of the Rest

Pretty village of Plockton

 Plockton
MAP D3

Prime candidate for the title of Scotland's prettiest west coast village, Plockton has sea, palm trees and a Rare Breeds Farm.

 Glen Affric
MAP D3

Glen Affric (see p28) is an example of nature's outstanding beauty, most easily accessed from the east at Cannich. At the western end, near Morvich, there's a walk to the breathtaking Falls of Glomach.

 Gairloch Heritage Museum
MAP C3 ▪ Gairloch ▪ (01445) 712 287 ▪ Open Mon–Sat ▪ Adm ▪ www. gairlochmuseum.org

Housed within an old nuclear bunker, this revamped museum has superb displays on the local land and people; the star exhibit being the Poolewe Hoard, a stash of Bronze Age artifacts discovered in 1877. Look out, too, for the "midgeater", an ingenious contraption designed to repel midges.

 Dunrobin Castle
MAP C4 ▪ Golspie ▪ (01408) 633 177 ▪ Open Apr–Oct ▪ Adm

A home befitting its wealthy landowners, the dukes of Sutherland. Towers, turrets and a palatial interior upon which no expense has been spared. Garden falconry displays too.

 The Hydroponicum, Achiltibuie
MAP C3 ▪ (01854) 622 202 ▪ Call ahead to book a visit ▪ Adm ▪ www.thehydroponicum.com

The glasshouse here (see p49) is known for cultivating various plants.

 Ullapool
MAP C3

Delightful grid-plan village with Gaelic street names, boat trips, ferries to the Western Isles, a museum and the dream-world Assynt Mountains. Visit Corrieshalloch Gorge en route.

 The Road to Applecross
MAP D2

To get to this small coastal village, you'll drive on pure adrenaline – the road climbs 750 m (2,000 ft) in steep zigzags to the Bealach na Bà (Pass of the Cattle). The scenery – with views across to Isle of Skye – is magnificent, and from here the more gradual descent into Applecross begins.

 Timespan
MAP C5 ▪ Helmsdale ▪ (01431) 821 327 ▪ Open Apr–Sep: 10am–5pm daily ▪ Adm ▪ www.timespan.org.uk

Well worth a visit to understand the effect of the 19th-century Clearances, which even today is visible throughout the north.

 Dornoch Cathedral
MAP C4

Madonna chose it for her wedding and 16 earls of Sutherland requested it for their burials; Dornoch is an impressive 13th-century cathedral (now the parish church).

 Loch Morar
MAP E3 ▪ www.lochmorar. org.uk

This enormous loch is 18 km (12 miles) long and offers great fishing, walking and wildlife watching – otters, sea eagles and golden eagles, and (reputedly) its own monster, Morag.

Places to Eat and Drink

1 Inverlochy Castle
MAP E3 ■ Torlundy, Fort William ■ (01397) 702 177 ■ £££
Many culinary awards have been bestowed upon the restaurant of this prestigious hotel. It features three dining rooms, a lavish set menu (of modern British cuisine) and a lengthy wine list.

2 Old Pines
MAP E3 ■ Spean Bridge ■ (01397) 712 324 ■ ££
Conscientiously organic, devoted to sourcing local ingredients and a member of the "slow food" movement, this little restaurant has earned a big name.

3 Airds Hotel
MAP E3 ■ Port Appin, Appin ■ (01631) 730 236 ■ £££
A country hotel restaurant with crisp, white table linen and candlelight, and a reputation for serving the best of Scottish produce.

4 The Mustard Seed
MAP D4 ■ 16 Fraser St, Inverness ■ (01463) 220 220 ■ ££
With its stylish interior and riverside location, the Mustard Seed produces some of the finest modern Scottish cuisine in the Highlands.

5 Applecross Inn
MAP D2 ■ Applecross, Wester Ross ■ (01520) 744 262 ■ ££
Spectacularly located beyond Britain's highest mountain pass, this pub overlooks Isle of Skye. Local seafood is served, and there is also live music some evenings.

6 Summer Isles Hotel
MAP C3 ■ Achiltibuie, Ross-shire ■ (01854) 622 282 ■ ££
Enjoy a relaxed atmosphere while dining at the bar, which is dog-friendly. The restaurant serves more formal meals. Sample dishes such as monkfish tail with bacon, or baked halibut with parmesan crumb.

PRICE CATEGORIES
For a three-course meal for one with half a bottle of wine (or equivalent meal), taxes and extra charges.

£ under £30 ££ £30–60 £££ over £60

7 The Ceilidh Place
MAP C3 ■ 14 West Argyle St, Ullapool ■ (01854) 612 103 ■ ££
Hotel-restaurant-bar and vibrant entertainment venue. Everything from a snack to a feast, plus live music and dance aplenty.

8 Clachaig Inn
MAP E3 ■ Glencoe ■ (01855) 811 252 ■ www.clachaig.com ■ ££
A legendary haunt of walkers, this hotel offers a wide range of food but is best known for its bar. Clachaig Inn is as essential to Highland trekkers as a first Munro.

9 Plockton Shores
MAP D3 ■ 30 Harbour St, Plockton ■ (01599) 544 263 ■ ££
The fruits of the west coast are served up with love and aplomb, on the shores of beautiful Loch Carron.

10 Crannog Seafood Restaurant
MAP E3 ■ Town Pier, Fort William ■ (01397) 705 589 ■ www.crannog.net ■ ££
Fresh seafood, a panoramic loch view and generous helpings. The atmosphere is welcoming, with efficient service. Reservations are essential.

Crannog Seafood Restaurant

See map on p116

TOP 10 West Coast Islands

More than 600 islands lie scattered along Scotland's Atlantic coastline, from seabird-clustered eyots to the landmasses of Skye, Mull, Lewis and Harris. The West Coast Islands represent escapism at its best and amply repay the effort of reaching them with the dramatic landscapes and hospitality of island folk. Regular ferries run all year, and special "island-hopping" fares are available.

Celtic cross, Islay

WEST COAST ISLANDS

0 km   40
0 miles   40

Port of Ness
North Tolsta
Isle of Lewis
Lochinver
Stornoway
Hushinish
Tarbert
Ullapool
Tigharry
Uig
Kinlochewe
Portree
Dunvegan
Stilligarry
Daliburgh
Skye
Kyle of Lochalsh
Barra
Small Isles
Inverie
Arisaig
Ardmolich
Coll
Tobermory
Iona and Staffa
Isle of Mull
Colonsay and Oronsay
Jura
Sanaigmore
Craighouse
Islay
Machrihanish

Outer Hebrides
Inner Hebrides
The Minch
The Little Minch
North Channel

1 Top 10 Sights
see pp122–5

1 Places to Eat and Drink
see p127

1 The Best of the Rest
see p126

1 Islay
MAP F2–G2 ■ Tourist info: (01496) 305 165

A thriving island with nine distilleries (see pp62–3) producing peaty malts. Bowmore, the island's capital, has an unusual circular church, designed to deprive the devil of corners in which to hide. Britain's most impressive 8th-century Celtic cross can be found at Kildalton. More than 250 species of birds have been spotted on Islay's varied landscapes.

2 Jura
MAP F2 ■ Tourist info: (01496) 305 165

The wildest and least visited of all the Hebridean islands. Overrun by red deer and dominated by its central hills, the Paps, Jura has been little affected by modernity: a single road links the ferry port and the main settlement, Craighouse. If you revel in solitude and rugged scenery, the walks are tremendous.

Red deer, Jura

Colourful seafront houses of Tobermory, Mull

3 Mull

MAP E2–F2 ■ Tourist info: (01680) 812 377; www.isle-of-mull.net

Matching Skye for beauty if not for size, Mull is the second largest of the Inner Hebrides. First port of call should be the imperious 13th-century Duart Castle, home to the chief of clan Maclean. A tour of the island must include side trips to Iona and Staffa, and Calgary Beach will stop you in your tracks. Tobermory is the place to unwind – its colourful seafront is a classic postcard scene. The Mishish pub there often has live music.

4 Colonsay and Oronsay

MAP F2 ■ Tourist info: Bowmore, Islay; (01496) 305 165

Colonsay has provided farmland and shelter to people since at least the Bronze Age, and many of their tombs and standing stones remain. Old traditions persist here, and Colonsay is still a strong crofting (see p124) and fishing community. Wild flowers and birds thrive on this terrain, but it is the coastline, with its mix of sprawling and secretive beaches, that lures most visitors. Check the tides and walk out to the adjacent little island of Oronsay, with its ruined priory; its Christian roots go back as far as Iona's.

5 Iona and Staffa

MAP F2–E2 ■ Boats for Staffa leave from Fionnphort; www.staffa tours.com ■ Tourist info: Mull (01680) 812 377

A sparkling island of white-sand beaches, Iona has an active crofting community. Many visitors come daily in summer to visit the famous restored abbey where St Columba came in 563 to establish a missionary centre (see p38); 48 Scottish kings are said to be buried here. Staffa contains Scotland's greatest natural wonder: Fingal's Cave, formed by thousands of basalt columns, which inspired German composer Felix Mendelssohn to pen his famous Hebrides Overture.

Altar inside the Iona Abbey

6 Coll
MAP E2 ■ Tourist info: Mull;
(01680) 812 377

Wild flowers, migrant birds, otters,
standing stones, active crofts, a
castle and a surfeit of beaches con-
tribute to making this a particularly
varied and delightful island.

Breachacha Castle, Coll

7 Small Isles
MAP D2–E2 ■ Tourist info:
Fort William; (01397) 701 801

While Canna and Muck are home
to traditional farming communities,
Rum was once the private play-
ground of a rich industrialist; you
can see his incredible fantasy home,
Kinloch Castle, as well as wander
the island's towering mountains.
Eigg was a landmark community
buyout, and the islander-owners
now run a crafts shop and tours.
Their ceilidhs (see p43) are legendary. The Sgurr of Eigg, a sugarloaf
spur, yields fabulous views.

CROFTING

Crofts are unique to the Highlands
and Islands. They are small parcels of
agricultural land, worked in addition
to other sources of income. There
are around 17,000 today, and grants
now ensure their continuation. But in
the mid-19th century, crofters were
denied basic rights and suffered great
abuse and hardship at the hands of
unscrupulous landlords.

8 Isle of Lewis
MAP C2 ■ Tourist info:
Stornoway; (01851) 703 088

Although geographically one island,
the northern half is called Lewis
and, the southern half, Harris.
Together, they are world-famous
for producing tweed. One thing
you absolutely must see is the
spectacular 4,500-year-old stone
circle known as the Callanish
(Calanais) Stones, which resonates
with a deep sense of mystery.
Arnol has an engaging traditional
"blackhouse" (blackened by smoke)
and Carloway, the ruined walls of
a remarkable Iron Age broch. Harris
is more mountainous. Driving the
"Golden Road" reveals the best
scenery; stop at the stunning
Luskentyre beach, with its miles of
white sands and blue-green water.

**Callanish Stones,
Isle of Lewis**

Plane on Cockle Beach, Barra

⑨ Barra
MAP D1 ■ Tourist info: Stornoway; (01851) 703 088

This small isle encapsulates all the charm of the Hebrides: scintillating beaches, the culture of the Gaels, tranquillity and road-priority to sheep. No matter how you arrive, it will make a deep impression: planes land on the sands of Cockle Beach, while ferries sail into a delightful bay where the 11th-century Kisimul Castle poses on an island of its own. A soothing place to unwind.

⑩ Isle of Skye
Mountainous, misty and magical, Skye *(see pp26–7)* is an island of dramatic scenery, with an ancient castle, an idolized distillery and plenty more attractions.

TWO DAYS AROUND MULL

▶ MORNING

Leave **Oban** *(see p106)* on a mid-morning ferry for the 45-minute trip across to the **Isle of Mull** *(see p123)*. Book your tickets ahead *(0800 066 5000; www.calmac.co.uk)*.

You might want to spend the day on a wildlife tour, as the island is home to sea eagles, otters and red deer. Mull Wildlife, for instance, can meet you off the ferry. Otherwise head for Duart Castle, 13th-century home of the Macleans (you can buy a combined ferry, bus and castle ticket from Calmac in Oban). After exploring the castle and gardens, have lunch in their delightfully quaint tearoom.

AFTERNOON

There are plenty of options for walks on Mull or you can drive to Calgary Bay to see the stunning white shell beach. Alternatively, make for Tobermory, the picture-postcard fishing port that is the island's main town. There are plenty of places to eat and to stay.

MORNING

Set off early to get to Fionnphort, to catch the 9:45am boat trip to **Staffa** *(see p123)*, where you can see **Fingal's Cave** *(see p70)* and the island's famous puffins. You'll be back within 3 hours, and can then pick up the quick ferry to the magical island of **Iona** *(see p123)*. Visit the **Abbey** *(see p56)*, wander its shores and enjoy its serenity. Return in time to catch the last ferry *(usually 7:15pm but check timetable in advance of travelling)* from Craignure back to Oban.

See map on p122 ←

The Best of the Rest

1 Arran
MAP G3 ■ Tourist info: (01770) 303 774

Long a favourite of Glaswegians, Arran is often described as "Scotland in miniature". Goat Fell is its craggy core, while the surrounds of Brodick Castle offer more forest-path walks.

2 Tiree
MAP E1 ■ Tourist info: Mull (01680) 812 377

Well-established on the surfers' circuit, this flat island not only has some of the finest Atlantic rollers on its beaches, but also claims the highest number of sunshine hours in the whole of Britain.

3 The Uists and Benbecula
MAP C1–D1 ■ Tourist info: Stornoway (01851) 703 088

A string of islands connected by causeways, with huge expanses of beaches on the west and rocky mountains on the east. This is also a wonderful trout fishing area.

4 Gigha
MAP G2 ■ www.gigha.org.uk

An exceptionally fertile island ("Isle of God"), which produces gourmet cheeses and tender plants and flowers, especially in the much-acclaimed Achamore Garden.

5 Lismore
MAP E3 ■ Tourist info: Oban (01631) 563 122

Situated in splendid scenery, this once important church island is now a quiet holiday retreat. Green and fertile, its name is said to mean "great garden".

6 Easdale
MAP E3 ■ Nr Oban ■ Tourist info: (01631) 563 122 ■ www.easdale.org

This former slate quarry has been transformed into a picturesque village. Surrounded by holes and fragmented rocks, it is a living museum.

7 Summer Isles
MAP C3 ■ Tourist info: Ullapool (01854) 612 486

The Summer Isles are a small cluster of islands in Loch Broom. It offers solitude and stupendous views of the arena of the Coigach mountains.

8 Kerrera
MAP E3 ■ Tourist info: Oban (01631) 563 122

A popular place for yachts to berth, this green, hilly island is ideal for walking, with clear views to Mull and the finest outlook on Oban.

9 Eriskay
MAP D1 ■ Tourist info: (01851) 703 088

The real-life scene of the *Whisky Galore* wreck in 1941, this is the dream island of the Hebrides. With beaches, crofts, hills – everything is just how the romantic would have it.

10 Luing
MAP F3 ■ Nr Isle of Seil ■ Bicycle hire: (01852) 314 274 ■ www.isleofluing.org

As it is not famous for anything other than its defunct slate quarry, you should have this isle to yourself. Pretty, and easy to tour by bicycle, it makes a perfect day trip from Oban.

Lismore Lighthouse

Places to Eat and Drink

PRICE CATEGORIES
For a three-course meal for one with half
a bottle of wine (or equivalent meal),
taxes and extra charges.

£ under £30 ££ £30–60 £££ over £60

1 Three Chimneys
MAP D2 ■ Colbost, Dunvegan,
Skye ■ (01470) 511 258 ■ www.three
chimneys.co.uk ■ £££

Since opening in 1985, this sublime
cottage restaurant *(see p65)* has
embraced its remote location, to
create a romantic setting with an
international reputation.

2 Digby Chick
MAP B2–C2 ■ 5 Bank St,
Stornoway, Isle of Lewis ■ (01851)
700 026 ■ www.digbychick.co.uk ■ ££

Bustling, child-friendly bistro by day;
candle-lit restaurant by night. Making
the most of fresh local seafood and
top-quality Scottish steak, book ahead
for the good-value early bird menu.

3 Langass Lodge
MAP C1 ■ Loch Eport, Isle
of North Uist ■ (01876) 580 285
■ www.langasslodge.co.uk ■ ££

One of the finest dining experiences
in the Hebrides. The magical menu
takes in the freshest of local seafood,
game and beef.

4 The Douglas Bistro
MAP G3 ■ Isle of Arran
■ (01770) 302 968 ■ ££

This restaurant offers a modern yet
classic take on bistro-style dining.
It serves delicious steaks and local
seafood, complemented by the
superb island views.

5 Jura Hotel
MAP F2 ■ Craighouse, Jura
■ (01496) 820 243 ■ www.jurahotel.
co.uk ■ ££

A quaint coastal hotel, where on any
given evening you are likely to meet
most of Jura's inhabitants. Simple food
served in the scenery of the gods.

6 Scarista House
MAP C1 ■ Sgarasta Bheag, Isle
of Harris ■ (01859) 550 238 ■ www.
scaristahouse.com ■ ££

Simple restaurant with a compact
and bijou menu. The food is sensational and the view is stunning.

Scarista House

7 Gannet Restaurant
MAP E2 ■ Coll Hotel, Ariangour,
Coll ■ (01879) 230 334 ■ www.
collhotel.com ■ ££

Waterfront restaurant serving fresh
seafood landed on the island. Try
the local mussels in garlic and
white wine or the roasted halibut.

8 The Mishnish
MAP E2 ■ Main St, Tobermory,
Mull ■ (01688) 302 500 ■ www.
themishnish.co.uk ■ ££

Celebrated pub on Tobermory's
seafront that attracts locals and
tourists alike for the live music.

9 Kinloch Lodge Hotel
MAP D2–3 ■ Sleat, Skye
■ (01471) 833 333 ■ www.kinloch-
lodge.co.uk ■ £££

Enjoy a five-course set dinner menu
featuring Black Isle lamb or local
sea trout at this delightful hotel.

10 Café Fish
MAP E2 ■ Tobermory, Mull
■ (01688) 301 253 ■ www.thecafefish.
com ■ ££

Popular bistro located on the pier
where much of its seafood is landed.
Produce is locally sourced and the
bread is homemade.

See map on p122

🔟 The Far North

Don't let the remoteness of the Far North deter you, for it is the emptiness itself that bestows upon the visitor a sense of wonder. The dazzling beaches along the northern coastline are a surprise to many, while further north still are the former Viking strongholds of Orkney and Shetland. Orkney contains one of the greatest concentrations of prehistoric remains in Europe, today grouped together as the Heart of Neolithic Orkney UNESCO World Heritage Centre. Shetland, on the other hand, is a much wilder frontier, festooned with millions of seabirds, and islanders who celebrate their Viking roots with a blazing fire festival, Up Helly Aa.

Great skua, Handa Island

THE FAR NORTH

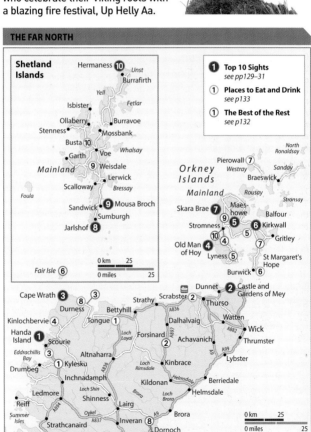

❶	**Top 10 Sights** see pp129–31
①	**Places to Eat and Drink** see p133
①	**The Best of the Rest** see p132

Shetland Islands

Hermaness ❿ Unst
Burrafirth
Yell
Isbister · Fetlar
Ollaberry · Burravoe
Stenness · Mossbank
Busta ❿
Garth · Voe · Whalsay
Mainland ❾ Weisdale
Lerwick
Scalloway · Bressay
Foula
Sandwick ❾ Mousa Broch
Sumburgh
Jarlshof ❽

Fair Isle ⑥

Pierowall ⑦
Orkney Westray · Sanday
Islands Braeswick
Mainland Rousay
North Ronaldsay
Skara Brae ⑦ Maes-
howe Balfour
Stromness ❾ ❺ ❻ Kirkwall
Old Man ❹ Lyness ❺ St Margaret's
of Hoy Burwick ⑥ Hope
Stronsay
Gritley ⑦

Cape Wrath ❸ ③
Durness ❽
Kinlochbervie ❹ Tongue ❶ Bettyhill
Handa ❶ Scourie Loch Loyal Forsinard ②
Island
Eddrachillis ③ Altnaharra
Bay ❶ Kylesku
Drumbeg Inchnadamph Loch Kinbrace
Ledmore Loch Shin Rimsdale Kildonan
Reiff Shinness Brora Loch Berriedale
Summer Oykel Lairg Brora Helmsdale
Isles Inveran
Strathcanaird Brora
Dornoch ❽

Dunnet ② Castle and
Scrabster ② Gardens of Mey
Strathy Thurso
Dalhalvaig Watten
Achavanich Wick
Thrumster
Lybster

0 km 25
0 miles 25

1 Handa Island
MAP B3 ■ Ferry: (07780) 967 800 ■ Scottish Wildlife Trust: www.scottishwildlifetrust.org.uk

Once populated by a hardy people who elected a queen and ran their own parliament, Handa was evacuated when the potato crop failed in 1847. Now it is a fantastic colony of seabirds that live here. Of particular note are the belligerent arctic and great skuas, kittiwakes, razorbills and the largest assembly of guillemots – numbering 66,000 – in Britain. A ferry (Apr–Aug: Mon–Sat) from Tarbet will take you to this island.

2 Castle and Gardens of Mey
MAP B5 ■ A836 Thurso–John O'Groats ■ (01847) 851 473 ■ Adm ■ www.castleofmey.org.uk

On the windswept Caithness coast is the UK's most northerly mainland castle, the Castle of Mey. Since 1952, the late Queen Elizabeth, the Queen Mother, lovingly restored the castle and gardens – her own personal taste is very apparent. The castle and grounds are now in trust for the benefit of the people of Caithness.

3 Cape Wrath
MAP B3 ■ Ferry: (07719) 678 729; open May–Sep

This is the most northwesterly point on the British mainland. Perched high on a clifftop stands a Stevenson light-

Cape Wrath Lighthouse

house (1827); below, the ocean pounds the rocks in a mesmerizing display of the Atlantic's strength. At Clo Mor, 8 km (5 miles) eastwards, are the highest cliffs on mainland Britain at 281 m (900 ft). The cape is reached by ferry from Keoldale Pier on Kyle of Durness, and a minibus runs to the lighthouse in summer.

4 Old Man of Hoy, Orkney
MAP A5 ■ Bike hire: www.orkneycyclehire.co.uk

This sandstone pinnacle rising 137 m (449 ft) from the sea is the most famous stack in Britain. It seems to change colour constantly as the light varies, and never fails to mesmerize. The Scrabster–Stromness ferry deviates to give passengers a view, but its best angle is from land. Hire bikes at Stromness and cycle to Rackwick Bay (on the way visit the Dwarfie Stane, a hollow rock), then it's a 2-hour round trip on foot.

Old Man of Hoy, seen from the westernmost point of Hoy, Orkney

The Neolithic cairn of Maeshowe on Orkney

5 Maeshowe, Orkney
MAP A5 ▪ (01856) 851 266
▪ Open Apr–Sep: 9:30am–5:30pm daily; Oct–Mar: 10am–4pm daily (guided tours only, book in advance)
▪ Adm (free for HES members)

This magnificent stone burial chamber, built around 2700 BC, is a World Heritage Site. Stoop low and walk through the entrance tunnel, carefully aligned with the solstice sun, and enter the greatest concentration of Viking graffiti ever discovered. Norsemen plundered the treasure but left the walls with a wealth of runes describing the kind of boasts and grumbles that people still make today.

6 Kirkwall, Orkney
MAP A5 ▪ Tourist info: (01856) 872 856 ▪ Palaces: (01856) 871 918; open Apr–Oct; adm ▪ Museum: (01856) 873 535

The capital of Orkney is a town of twisted streets, ancient buildings and the constant comings and goings of ferries. Most striking is the enormous red and yellow St Magnus's Cathedral, built in the 12th century and still going strong. Nearby are the ruins of the bishop's and earl's palaces. The town museum is excellent, and many shops in the city sell an extensive range of Orcadian jewellery.

7 Skara Brae, Orkney
MAP A5 ▪ (01856) 841 815
▪ Open Apr–Sep: 9:30am–5:30pm daily; Oct–Mar: 10am–4pm daily
▪ Adm (free for HES members)

Another World Heritage Site, one that predates the Egyptian pyramids. In 1850, a storm revealed some ruins in the sands, whereupon archaeologists excavated and were astonished to find a 5,000-year-old Stone Age village, which had been abandoned so suddenly that most of the rooms and furnishings were left intact. Today, you can see the stone beds and sideboards of these Neolithic people, and discover how and what they cooked. A visitor centre explains.

8 Jarlshof, Shetland
MAP B1 ▪ (01950) 460 112
▪ Open Apr–Sep: 9:30am–5:30pm daily (Oct–Mar: call for open times)
▪ Adm (free for HES members)

This warren of underground (but roofless) chambers represents not one but at least five periods of settlement. The oval-shaped houses are Bronze Age; the Iron Age added the broch and wheelhouses; the Picts established their own dwellings; the Vikings erected long houses, and a farm was created in medieval times. This archaeological site, close to the soaring bird-cliffs of Sumburgh Head, is exceptional.

Jarlshof, Shetland

⑨ Mousa Broch, Shetland

MAP B2 ■ Boat trips:
(07901) 872 339; open Apr–Sep
daily (weather permitting); www.
mousa.co.uk

Around 500 BC the Iron Age people
began building defensive forts called
brochs. Masterfully designed, these
double-skinned walls of dry stones
were raised into circular towers,
with an elegant taper at their waists.
Remains of brochs are scattered
across northern Scotland but Mousa
is the best preserved. You can only
reach it by boat, and then must climb
13 m (43 ft) to the open parapet.

Mousa Broch, Shetland

⑩ Hermaness National Nature Reserve, Shetland

MAP A2 ■ Unst ■ (0463) 667 600
■ Best visiting times: mid-May–late Jul
■ www.nature.scot

When you look from here to Muckle
Flugga lighthouse, you're gazing at
the northernmost tip of Britain. Aside
from the view, the cliff-edged reserve
is a favourite breeding ground for
bonxies (great skuas). Alongside these
pirates (they steal food from other
seabirds), there are gannets, razorbills,
red-throated divers and a large
gathering of tammy nories (puffins).

A DAY ON ORKNEY

▶ **MORNING**

Start the morning from the
flagstoned village of **Stromness**
(see p132) and head out on the
road to **Skara Brae**. The roads
turn and undulate on rolling pasture but the way is well signposted, which is a pity as Orkney is a
delightful place to get lost in.

You'll need 2 hours to do the
Neolithic remains justice, as
well as fitting in a visit to Skaill
House and stocking up on sweet
treats such as fudge and ice
cream in the shop.

Drive on to the great ancient
stone circle known as the **Ring
of Brodgar** *(see p132)*, and also
visit the roadside standing
stones of Stenness.

So far you've only covered 20 km
(12 miles). Time for lunch as you
make your way to the Maeshowe
Visitor Centre.

AFTERNOON

After lunch, take a tour inside
Neolithic **Maeshowe**. It's dark
inside, and a guide lights up
the runes with a torch. Drive
on to **Kirkwall**. Visit the cathedral and the museum, and
walk the town's charming
streets, or stop for a coffee.

In the evening, dine at
The Storehouse Restaurant
*(Map A5, Bridge Street Wynd,
01856 252 250)*.

Orkney is also a delightful
place to cycle and it's easy
to hire bicycles. The car
route described above
makes a lovely day's cycle
ride if you return to Stromness
after Maeshowe.

See map on p128 ←

The Best of the Rest

(1) Eas A'Chual Aluinn Fall, nr Kylesku

MAP B3 ▪ Take a boat from Kylesku; (07821) 441 090; open Mar–Oct

Eas A'Chual Aluinn is Britain's highest waterfall. It drops 200 m (658 ft) at the end of Loch Glencoul.

(2) Forsinard Flows

MAP B4 ▪ (01641) 571 225 ▪ Visitor centre: open Apr–Oct ▪ www.rspb.org.uk

The great peatland, known as the Flow Country, offers walks among rare plants, insects and birds.

(3) Smoo Cave, Durness

MAP B4 ▪ Apr–Oct ▪ www.smoocavetours.com

Remarkable natural cavern beside the sea. You can walk in a little way, but a boat tour is best.

(4) Pier Arts Centre, Stromness

MAP A5 ▪ www.pierartscentre.com

There is a collection of British fine art here. Most works were created in the 1930s and 1940s by avant-garde artists.

(5) Scapa Flow Visitor Centre, Hoy, Orkney

MAP A5 ▪ (01856) 873 535 ▪ Reopening Jul 2022 ▪ www.orkney.gov.uk

An exploration of the bay of Scapa Flow, where, in 1919, the German High Seas Fleet scuttled their 74 warships after surrendering to the Royal Navy.

(6) Fair Isle, Shetland

MAP B1 ▪ www.fairisle.org.uk

Famous as a haven of traditional crafts, this remote island has awesome cliff scenery and birdlife (from May to mid-August, puffins are the big draw). The ferry is weather-dependent, so be prepared for a wait.

Façade of the Italian Chapel, Orkney

(7) Churchill Barriers and Italian Chapel, Orkney

MAP A5 ▪ Lamb Holm, nr Kirkwall ▪ Chapel: open Nov–Mar: 10am–1pm daily (Apr & Oct: to 4pm); May & Sep 9am–5pm daily (Jun–Aug: to 6:30pm) ▪ Adm

These causeways were built in World War II by Italian prisoners of war, who also built the picturesque chapel.

(8) Dornoch

MAP C4

This attractive market town features a 13th-century cathedral, a museum of local history, plenty of shops and cafés as well as a long sandy beach.

(9) Ring of Brodgar, Orkney

MAP A5 ▪ Nr Stromness ▪ www.historicenvironment.scot

An atmospheric prehistoric site of 36 slabs raised to form a circle. There are taller (but fewer) standing stones nearby at Stenness.

A puffin catches dinner, Fair Isle

(10) Stromness, Orkney

MAP A5 ▪ Tourist info: www.stromnessorkney.com

Stromness is a charming town of flagstone streets with a museum that draws on the Orcadian connection with the Hudson Bay Shipping Company.

Places to Eat and Drink

PRICE CATEGORIES

For a three-course meal for one with half a bottle of wine (or equivalent meal), taxes and extra charges.

£ under £30   **££** £30–60   **£££** over £60

1 Tongue Hotel
MAP B4 ■ Tongue ■ (01847) 611 206 ■ ££

A characterful old hotel, the low prices of which belie the quality of Highland fare served. The best of local produce is used with imagination and flair.

2 The Captain's Galley
MAP B5 ■ The Harbour, Scrabster ■ (01847) 894 999 ■ Closed Sun & Mon ■ £££

Stylish restaurant in an exposed-brick former ice house. Serves all different kinds of fish, fresh from the morning's catch. Book in advance.

3 Eddrachilles Hotel, Scourie
MAP B3 ■ Badcall Bay, Scourie ■ (01971) 502 080 ■ ££

Among trees on a ragged coastline, this fine old hotel has a stone-walled dining room where local sourced food is served. A long conservatory, too, for catching the sun.

4 Kinlochbervie Hotel
MAP B3 ■ Kinlochbervie ■ (01971) 521 275 ■ £

Somewhat stark, but it more than makes up for it with its good views and simple value-for-money food. Hill lamb, venison, salmon and local seafood are favourites. Good wines.

5 The Foveran
MAP B5 ■ St Ola, Kirkwall ■ (01856) 872 389 ■ Times vary, check website ■ www.thefoveran. com ■ ££

Renowned restaurant serving dishes such as fillet of Orkney steak and North Ronaldsay mutton. It offers great views over Scapa Flow.

6 The Skerries Bistro
MAP B5 ■ Nr Burwick ■ (01856) 831 605 ■ Closed Sat ■ ££

Set in a glass building with superb views of the Pentland Firth, this lovely restaurant serves local produce such as hand-dived scallops and Orkney lobster.

7 Pierowall Hotel, Orkney
MAP A5 ■ Pierowall, Westray ■ (01857) 677 472 ■ £

Come here for the best fish and chips in the isles. Otherwise, nothing particularly fancy, but simple home cooking and plenty of choice.

8 Cocoa Mountain
MAP B3 ■ 8 Balnakeil, Durness ■ (01971) 511 233 ■ £

An unlikely location for a world-class chocolatier, but one not to miss. On offer are delicious artisan truffles and hot chocolate, as well as a selection of coffees and teas. A bonus is the beautiful views of Loch Criospol.

Chocolate truffles, Cocoa Mountain

9 Mill Café, Shetland
MAP B1 ■ Weisdale ■ (01595) 743 843 ■ Closed Mon ■ £

In this renovated old mill, combine the visual delights of the Bonhoga Gallery with delectable snacks: marinated herring, smoked salmon, organic quiches.

10 Busta House, Shetland
MAP A1 ■ Busta, Brae ■ (01806) 522 506 ■ ££

This historic Shetland hotel (see p151) also features a revered and reasonably priced restaurant. The tastiest lamb on the island is found here, along with seafood dishes, including particularly good scallops and halibut.

See map on p128

Streetsmart

Jeffrey Street and the roofs
of Old Town, Edinburgh

Getting Around

Arriving by Air

Scotland has five main international airports, with smaller regional airports located across the country. **Edinburgh International Airport** welcomes direct flights from the USA, Canada and Europe, and it also has domestic links to London and major cities in the UK. Connecting flights go to Orkney, Wick, Lewis, Islay and Shetland.

Edinburgh Airport is situated 11 km (7 miles) from the city, and buses ply regularly between the airport and the city centre. The Airlink 100 departs every 10 to 15 minutes and takes around 40 minutes to reach Edinburgh Waverley, the city's main train station. Tickets cost £4.50 one-way or £7.50 return. The X90 services connect the airport with Dundee eight times daily, taking around 80 minutes; tickets cost £14.

Regular trams also link the airport with the city centre. The journey time is 30 minutes, though tickets are a little more expensive at £6.50 one-way and £9 return. Getting to and from Edinburgh Airport by taxi is also a viable option.

Glasgow International Airport welcomes direct flights from Canada and the USA, and it has domestic links to London and other UK airports. Connecting flights go to Barra, Benbecula, Campbeltown, Orkney, Shetland, Islay, the Isle of Lewis and Tiree. Glasgow Airport is 13 km (8 miles) from the city centre. The Airport Express service 500 departs every 10 minutes, and takes 15 minutes. Tickets cost £9 for a one-way trip and £14.80 return. There is a direct bus to Skye via Loch Lomond and Fort William. Taxis are available, too.

Inverness is 15 km (9 miles) from the city centre. The airport has links with all the main European cities, and onward connections to Scotland's northern and western isles. Buses run every 30 minutes.

Dundee Airport is less than 2 km (1 mile) from the city centre and train station, and has flights from London and Belfast. There is a taxi rank at the terminal, but no public transport.

Aberdeen International Airport has direct links to many European destinations. Connecting routes go to Orkney, Shetland, Lewis and Wick. The airport is 11 km (7 miles) from Aberdeen city centre, and can be reached via the Jet 727 bus service within 30 minutes. Tickets cost £4 for a one-way trip or £5.70 return. Buses also run to Montrose and Stonehaven. Taxis are also available. The nearest train station is Dyce on the Aberdeen to Inverness Line.

International Train Travel

Edinburgh and Glasgow are the main hubs for rail travel between Scotland and the rest of the UK. There are connections at London St Pancras International for **Eurostar** services from mainland Europe. **London North Eastern Railway (LNER)** then runs from London to Edinburgh, Dundee and Aberdeen. **Avanti West Coast** operates from London Euston to Glasgow and onward to Edinburgh. Some trains continue to Inverness. The **Caledonian Sleeper** operates regular overnight services from London Euston to Glasgow, Edinburgh, Aberdeen, Inverness and Fort William. The **Interrail Great Britain Pass** offers a deal on travel throughout Scotland and the rest of the UK for 3, 4, 6 or 8 days within a month.

Long-Distance Bus Travel

Day and night **National Express** services operate out of major cities. Though reliable and much cheaper than trains, journeys by coach are longer. The main bus station in Edinburgh is just off St Andrew's Square; Glasgow's is located at the east end of Sauchiehall Street.

Megabus operates services from London Victoria to Glasgow (5 daily; 9 hours 30 minutes) and Edinburgh (2 daily; 8 hours 30 minutes).

Boats and Ferries

There is no ferry service between Scotland and continental Europe, but **P&O** sails between Hull, Rotterdam and Zeebrugge, and **DFDS Seaways** sails between Newcastle and Amsterdam. Ferry services by **Stena Line** and **P&O** operate between Belfast and Larne to Cairnryan on the southwest coast.

For island hoppers, **Caledonian MacBrayne** offers passes valid for 8 days, 15 days or one month on its routes to the western isles including Arran, Barra, Coll, Eigg, Harris, Islay, Mull, Raasay, Skye and Tiree. **NorthLink Ferries** sails to Stromness in Orkney from Scrabster and from Aberdeen to Kirkwall in Orkney and Lerwick in Shetland. **Pentland Ferries** offers car ferries to South Ronaldsay in Orkney from Gill's Bay. **John O'Groats Ferries** is a passenger-only service to South Ronaldsay. **Hebridean Island Cruises** tour the Western Isles aboard the luxurious 30-cabin Hebridean Princess. **Caledonian Discovery** also

operates barge cruises on the Caledonian Canal and the lochs of the Great Glen.

Regional and Local Trains

Lines within Scotland are coordinated by **National Rail**, with main stations in Glasgow, Edinburgh, Stirling, Perth, Dundee, Aberdeen, Inverness, Fort William and Oban.

The West Highland Line, operated by **West Coast Railways**, runs between Glasgow and Mallaig and offers spectacular views.

The **Borders Railway** runs between Tweedbank and Edinburgh.

Tickets are available from **Trainline**, **National Rail** and **ScotRail**. ScotRail also offer rail passes with unlimited train travel for a certain number of days.

Public Transport

Scotland's public transport is a combination of private sector and city-operated services, and fares are relatively inexpensive compared to London and many European countries.

Most cities operate only bus systems. **Transport For Edinburgh** complement the city's bus system with a single tram line. In Glasgow, **Strathclyde Partnership for Transport (SPT)** run a comprehensive bus service, a single subway circuit and a sub-urban rail network.

Traveline Scotland provides the latest ticket information, timetables and safety and hygiene measures for all public transport services across the country, as well as live updates on local services.

DIRECTORY

ARRIVING BY AIR

Aberdeen International Airport
w aberdeenairport.com

Dundee Airport
w hial.co.uk/
dundee-airport

Edinburgh International Airport
w edinburghairport.com

Glasgow International Airport
w glasgowairport.com

Inverness Airport
w hial.co.uk/
inverness-airport

INTERNATIONAL TRAIN TRAVEL

Avanti West Coast
w avantiwestcoast.co.uk

Caledonian Sleeper
w sleeper.scot

Eurostar
w eurostar.com

Interrail Great Britain Pass
w interrail.eu

London North Eastern Railway (LNER)
w lner.co.uk

LONG-DISTANCE BUS TRAVEL

Megabus
w uk.megabus.com

National Express
w nationalexpress.com

BOATS AND FERRIES

Caledonian Discovery
w caledonian-discovery.co.uk

Caledonian MacBrayne
w calmac.co.uk

DFDS Seaways
w dfds.com

Hebridean Island Cruises
w hebridean.co.uk

John O'Groats Ferries
w jogferry.co.uk

NorthLink Ferries
w northlinkferries.co.uk

P&O
w poferries.com

Pentland Ferries
w pentlandferries.co.uk

Stena Line
w stenaline.co.uk

REGIONAL AND LOCAL TRAINS

Borders Railway
w bordersrailway.co.uk

National Rail
w nationalrail.co.uk

Scotrail
w scotrail.co.uk

Trainline
w thetrainline.com

West Coast Railways
w westcoastrailways.co.uk

PUBLIC TRANSPORT

SPT
w spt.co.uk

Transport For Edinburgh
w transportfor
edinburgh.com

Traveline Scotland
w travelinescotland.com

Bus

The largest bus provider is **Scottish Citylink**, which connects major towns and cities. If you are looking to see the sights, **Rabbie's Trail Burners** and **MacBackpackers** are two well-reputed minibus and hostel tour companies.

Urban bus networks are generally fast, frequent and reliable. In most cities, a single fare applies for all bus travel within city limits. Multiple trip tickets and one-day travel passes are available in most major cities. These can be purchased online and stored on your phone. Single-trip tickets can also be bought from the driver when boarding your bus, but change is not given so you must pay the exact fare.

Public transport in rural areas is less extensive. Timetables are usually designed around the needs of local workers and school students, so schedules tend to be much less convenient for visitors, with departures either very early in the morning, late in the afternoon or early evening.

Trams

Scotland's only tram line connects Edinburgh International Airport with the city centre, with stops on the way. There are plans to extend it as far as Leith and Newhaven by 2023.

Subway

Glasgow's SPT subway, the only underground rail service in Scotland, comprises a 10 km (7 mile) loop connecting 15 stations around the city centre. Trains run every 4 minutes at peak times, and it takes 24 minutes to ride a full loop. Tickets can be purchased from self-service machines at any subway station. Single tickets are a fixed price and are valid on any journey. Savings can be made by buying a return (£3.30) or an all-day pass (£4.20).

Taxi

Taxis are regulated and legally obliged to display a licence number. City taxis should be metered but unmetered cars operate in remote areas – ask for the fare before you get in. **City Cabs** in Edinburgh, **Rainbow City Taxis** in Aberdeen, **Glasgow Taxis**, **Inverness Taxis**, and **Dundee City Cab** are all recommended taxi services that can be booked in advance.

Cabs can be picked up at taxi ranks or hailed on the street. London-style black cabs display a yellow "taxi" sign which is lit up when the taxi is free. "Private hire" cars must be booked by phone. Taxi apps such as Uber and Bolt also operate in most Scottish cities.

Driving

The journey to Edinburgh or Glasgow from London or main English ferry ports via the M1 and M6 motorways takes around 8–9 hours. If arriving by car ferry to Newcastle the A1 brings you to Edinburgh in around 2.5 hours. Driving in Scottish cities is not recommended during your stay; traffic is heavy and parking scarce. However, travelling by car is the easiest way to explore beyond major cities. Roads are generally very good, with motorways or dual carriageways connecting most major towns and cities. In remote areas some roads are single carriageway, with designated passing places.

Be aware that weather can change rapidly and driving conditions can deteriorate suddenly at any time of year.

Car Rental

To rent a car in Scotland you must be at least 21 years old (some rental companies insist on a minimum age of 25) and have held a valid licence for at least one year. Major car rental agencies have outlets at airports and in major towns and cities.

Rules of the Road

If you are planning on driving during your stay, familiarize yourself with the rules of the road prior to getting behind the wheel of a vehicle.

Always drive on the left. Seat belts must be worn at all times and children must travel with the appropriate child restraint for their weight and size. Mobile telephones may not be used while driving, except with a handsfree system. Third party insurance is required by law.

Overtake on the outside or right-hand lane, and give priority to traffic approaching from the right. Always give way to emergency service vehicles. It is illegal to drive and park in bus lanes unless otherwise stated –

restrictions are signposted. On single-track roads which are wide enough for only one vehicle, pull into the nearest designated passing place on your left, or wait opposite a passing place on your right, to allow an oncoming vehicle to pass. You should also use passing places to allow drivers to overtake.

Scotland's legal alcohol limit for drivers is lower than the rest of the UK's, at 50 mg of alcohol per 100ml (0.05 per cent BAC). It is best to avoid drinking alcohol entirely if you plan to drive a vehicle.

In the event of a breakdown or accident, or if you require assistance on the road, contact the **AA**.

Cycling

The trails of the Highlands are perfect for off-road riding, and there are great networks for mountain bikers and gentle trails following old canal towpaths or former railway lines. Long-distance cycle routes and mountain bike trails are available on land owned by **Forestry and Land Scotland**.

7Stanes off-road trails span the entirety of southern Scotland. You can find traffic-free city and countryside bike routes on the website of the UK's National Cycle Network, **Sustrans**.

Bike transport is possible on most trains. Faster, long-distance services require pre-booking.

Off road, touring and city bikes, bikes for younger children, and electrically-assisted e-bikes can be rented from companies like **Biketrax** in Edinburgh and **EBS Cycle Centre** in Dundee. **Nextbike** is a cycle sharing scheme with 500 bikes available from more than 60 locations around Glasgow.

Several companies operate guided and self-guided bike tours around Scotland. **Wilderness Scotland** offers guided cycling tours in areas including the Cairngorms, the Hebrides and the Great Glen, with a support van to carry your luggage.

Walking and Hiking

Scotland is a fantastic destination for walkers and hikers. Check the **Scottish Mountaineering Club**, **Scotways** and **Ramblers** for specific route information.

Scotland's mountains are easy to reach but bad weather can strike at any time, so planning and good preparation is essential. Ensure you have good hiking boots, warm waterproof clothing, a map and a compass. Tell someone where you're going and when you plan to return.

Walking is also an enjoyable way to explore compact city centres such as Edinburgh, Glasgow and Stirling where key sites are generally within easy reach.

Practical Information

Passports and Visas

For entry requirements, including visas, consult your nearest British embassy or check the **Visas and Immigration** page on the UK government website. For a stay of up to three months, EU nationals and citizens of the US, Canada, Australia and New Zealand do not need a visa.

Government Advice

It is important to consult both your and the UK government's advice before travelling, and the **UK Foreign and Commonwealth Office**, the **US State Department**, and the **Australian Department of Foreign Affairs and Trade** offer the latest information and advice on security, health and local regulations.

Customs and Immigration

You can find information on the laws relating to goods and currency taken in or out of the UK on the **UK Government** website.

Insurance

We recommend that you take out a comprehensive insurance policy covering theft, loss of belongings, medical care, cancellations and delays, and read the small print carefully.

Health

Scotland, and the rest of the UK, has a world-class healthcare system.

Holders of the EU's European Health Insurance Card (EHIC) can receive medical treatment free of charge. Accident and emergency treatment is free to all and immediate payment for urgent treatment is not required.

For information regarding COVID-19 vaccination requirements, consult government advice.

If you have an accident or medical problem that requires non-urgent medical attention you can find details of the nearest non-emergency medical service on the **NHS** website. Alternatively, call the **NHS 24** helpline number at any hour on 111, or go to the nearest Accident and Emergency (A&E) department. Hospitals with 24-hour emergency services in Scotland include **University Hospital Ayr**, **Borders General Hospital** in Melrose, **Dumfries and Galloway Royal Infirmary**, **Aberdeen Royal Infirmary**, **Glasgow Royal Infirmary**, **Royal Infirmary of Edinburgh** and **Belford Hospital** in Fort William.

For minor ailments go to a pharmacy or chemist. You may need a prescription to obtain certain pharmaceuticals. The pharmacist can inform you of the closest doctor's surgery or medical centre.

Smoking, Alcohol and Drugs

Smoking and vaping are banned inside all public spaces such as bus, train stations and airports and in enclosed areas of bars, cafés and restaurants.

Alcohol may not be sold to or bought for anyone under 18 and may only be purchased between the hours of 10am and 10pm, and 12:30pm and 10pm on a Sunday. The drink-drive limit is strictly enforced (see p139).

Possession of all recreational drugs and psychoactive substances is a criminal offence.

ID

Visitors to the UK are not required to carry ID on their person at all times, however passports are required as ID at airports, even when taking internal flights within the UK. Anyone who looks under 18 may be asked for photo ID to prove their age when buying alcohol.

Personal Security

Scotland is generally safe, but petty crime does take place. Pickpockets work known tourist areas and busy streets such as Edinburgh's Royal Mile and Glasgow's Buchanan Street. Use your common sense and be alert to your surroundings. If you have anything stolen, report the crime as soon as possible at the nearest police station. Get a copy of the crime report in order to make a claim on your insurance later.

For emergency **police**, **fire**, **ambulance** services, or emergency **mountain rescue**, dial 999 (or 112). For medical help or non-emergency situations, dial 111. These numbers are free on any public phone.

Contact your embassy or consulate immediately if your passport is stolen or in the event of a serious crime or accident.

Scots are generally accepting of all people, regardless of their race, gender or sexuality.

LGBTQ+ rights are generally in line with the rest of the UK, which are considered among the most progressive in Europe. Same-sex marriage was legalized in Scotland in 2014 and Scotland became the first country in the world to include LGBTQ+ history and education in the school curriculum. Scotland's major cities have vibrant LGBTQ+ scenes, and since 2018 smaller towns and villages have launched their own Pride parades. Despite all the freedoms that the LGBTQ+ community enjoy, acceptance is not a given. **LGBT Helpline Scotland** is a fantastic service that provides support and practical information for victims of homophobic abuse or LGBTQ+ hate crimes.

Travellers with Specific Requirements

The Visit Scotland website has information for those visiting Scotland with specific requirements. Modern sights tend to be accessible, but historic buildings may not be. Phone ahead to check. **Capability Scotland** is Scotland's largest organization and **Tourism for All** is the UK's central source of travel information. **Disability Rights UK** lists accommodation. **Seagull Trust Cruises** runs canal boats that are specifically designed for the disabled on the Forth (Edinburgh) and Caledonian (Inverness) canals. Disabled parking bays are widespread but you must display a badge. The AA *(see p137)* produce a *Disabled Travellers' Guide* and have an **AA Disability Helpline** for members.

Other sources that offer useful advice are the **Royal National Institute for Deaf People** and the **Royal National Institute for the Blind**.

DIRECTORY

PASSPORTS AND VISAS

Visas and Immigration
w gov.uk/browse/visas-immigration

GOVERNMENT ADVICE

Australian Department of Foreign Affairs and Trade
w smartraveller.gov.au

UK Foreign and Commonwealth Office
w gov.uk/foreign-travel-advice

US Department of State
w travel.state.gov

CUSTOMS AND IMMIGRATION

UK Government
w gov.uk

HEALTH

Aberdeen Royal Infirmary
Foresterhill, Aberdeen
((0345) 456 6000

Belford Hospital
Belford Rd, Fort William
((01397) 702481

Borders General Hospital
Huntlyburn, Melrose
((01896) 826000

Dumfries and Galloway Royal Infirmary
Cargenbridge, Dumfries
((01387) 246246

Glasgow Royal Infirmary
84 Castle St
((0141) 211 4000

NHS
w nhs.uk

NHS 24
(111

Royal Infirmary of Edinburgh
51 Little France Crescent, Old Dalkeith Rd, Edinburgh
((0131) 536 1000

PERSONAL SECURITY

Ambulance, fire, police, mountain rescue
(999 (or 112)
(111 (non emergency)

LGBT Helpline
(0300 123 2523
w lgbthealth.org.uk

TRAVELLERS WITH SPECIFIC REQUIREMENTS

AA Disability Helpline
((0800) 262050

Capability Scotland
w capability.scot

Disability Rights UK
w disabilityrightsuk.org

Royal National Institute for the Blind
w rnib.org.uk

Royal National Institute for Deaf People
w rnid.org.uk

Seagull Trust Cruises
w seagulltrust.org.uk

Tourism for All
w tourismforall.org.uk

Time Zone

Scotland operates on Greenwich Mean Time (GMT) which is 1 hour behind Continental Europe Time and 5 hours ahead of US Eastern Seaboard Time. The clock advances 1 hour during "British Summer Time", spanning the last Sunday in March until the last Sunday in October.

Money

Britain's currency is pound sterling (£). Scottish notes are different to those used in the rest of the UK; as a result, they are occasionally not accepted elsewhere in the UK.

Major credit, debit and prepaid currency cards are accepted. Contactless payment is almost universal, including for almost all buses, all trains and taxis.

Cash machines are located at banks and on main streets in major towns, but they are harder to find in remote areas.

Tipping is not obligatory, but it is customary to leave a tip of 5–10 per cent if service is good.

Electrical Appliances

Power sockets are type G, fitting three-pronged plugs. Standard voltage is 230 volts.

Mobile Phones and Wi-Fi

Free Wi-Fi hotspots are widely available in city centres. Restaurants and cafés will usually give you their Wi-Fi password if you buy something.

Do not rely on mobile phones for navigation or emergency calls in rural areas as reception can be intermittent.

Visitors travelling to the UK with EU tariffs may be affected by data roaming charges now that the UK has left the EU. Check with your provider before travelling. Pay-as-you-go SIM cards can be bought in most supermarkets.

Postal Services

Standard post is handled by the **Royal Mail**. There are post offices throughout Scotland, some in supermarkets or other stores. Larger post offices will open from 9am to 5:30pm on weekdays and until 12:30pm on Saturdays. You can also buy stamps in shops.

Weather

Scotland has a highly variable weather pattern. The east is drier than the west, but rain can occur throughout the year, and heavy snowfalls are possible in winter.

In summer, Scotland enjoys longer days than the rest of the UK, and temperatures average 15–22° C (59–72° F); winter temperatures 1–7° C (34–45° F) and days are shorter. The **Met Office** website is a great resource for up-to-date, detailed forecasts.

Opening Hours

Most shops are open 9am–5:30pm Monday to Saturday. City shops are usually open until 8pm Thursday and many now open Sunday, too.

Museum and gallery times vary widely, so check ahead. Last admission to many attractions tends to be 30 minutes before closing.

Scotland has three main holiday periods: Hogmanay (New Year), Easter and July–August. National public holidays in Scotland differ slightly to the rest of the UK. They are 1–2 January, Good Friday (March/April), the first and last Monday in May, the first Monday in August, St Andrew's Day (Nov 30), Christmas day and Boxing day on 25–26 December.

The COVID-19 pandemic proved that situations can change suddenly. Always check before visiting attractions and hospitality venues for up-to-date hours and booking requirements.

Visitor Information

Visit Scotland provides good general information and has an excellent website – it's a great place to start planning your trip. Scotland's main visitor information centres are in Edinburgh and Glasgow, and there are also regional tourist offices, some open year-round, others open during the summer months only.

If you plan to visit many of the country's heritage sights, the **Historic Environment Scotland Explorer Pass** provides access to upwards of 70 attractions over a 3-, 7- or 14-day period.

For those planning to travel extensively within Scotland, Scotrail's **Spirit of Scotland pass** offers unlimited train, bus and ferry transport over an 8-or 15-day period.

The **Scottish Citylink Explorer Pass** offers 3-, 5-and 8-days unlimited travel on its extensive coach network, as well as discounts and special offers on accommodation.

National Trust members can use their access card for entry to heritage sights in Scotland that are looked after by the **National Trust for Scotland**.

Responsible Tourism

Scotland is home to some of the most accessible, open spaces in Europe. It is the law that every person, regardless of whether they are a local or a resident, should have access to the countryside in Scotland. As long as you act responsibly, you can walk, cycle, canoe and horse ride in all open land or waters. Be sure to familiarize yourself with the **Scottish Outdoor Access Code** before you set off on your trip.

Local Customs

Some remote areas of the Highlands and Islands are deeply religious. Be respectful when visiting places of worship.

Language

English is the main language in Scotland. Regional accents can sometimes be challenging, even for visitors from other Anglophone countries. Gaelic, Scotland's second official language, is now spoken by fewer than 1 per cent of the population, and it is most commonly spoken in the Outer Hebrides.

Taxes and Refunds

Stores offering tax-free shopping will display a distinctive sign and will provide non-EU residents with a VAT 407 form. This is validated when you leave the UK and allows you to reclaim value added tax (VAT) on certain products. VAT is charged on most goods and services and is included in the price.

Accommodation

Scotland offers a variety of accommodation, from luxury five-star hotels to family-run B&Bs, and budget hostels run by **Hostelling Scotland**. Prices are higher in the summer, especially in the Highlands and Islands and in Edinburgh during the festive season and Hogmanay (New Year).

Organizations such as **The Landmark Trust** and the **National Trust for Scotland Holidays** offer accommodation in lighthouses, castles and in historic properties.

The **Mountain Bothies Association** is a charity that looks after over 100 unlocked "bothies" (simple wooden or stone huts). Set in remote areas, they usually have a platform for sleeping, table, seats and a fireplace. They are free, but donations are welcome.

Camping is allowed almost anywhere, so long as you are respectful of the community and leave the site as you found it.

DIRECTORY

POSTAL SERVICES

Royal Mail
🌐 royalmail.com

WEATHER

Met Office
🌐 metoffice.gov.uk

VISITOR INFORMATION

Historic Environment Scotland Explorer Pass
🌐 historicenvironment.scot

Scottish Citylink Explorer Pass
🌐 citylink.co.uk

Spirit of Scotland
🌐 scotrail.co.uk

National Trust for Scotland
🌐 nts.org.uk

Visit Scotland
🌐 visitscotland.com

RESPONSIBLE TOURISM

Scottish Outdoor Access Code
🌐 outdooraccess-scotland.scot

ACCOMMODATION

The Landmark Trust
🌐 landmarktrust.org.uk

Mountain Bothies Association
🌐 mountainbothies.org.uk

National Trust for Scotland Holidays
🌐 nts.org.uk

Hostelling Scotland (HS)
🌐 hostellingscotland.org.uk

Places to Stay

PRICE CATEGORIES
For a standard, double room per night (with breakfast if included), taxes and extra charges.

£ under £100   ££ £100–200   £££ over £200

Edinburgh's Luxury Hotels

House of Gods
MAP N4 ■ 233 Cowgate ■ (0131) 230 0445 ■ www.houseofgodshotel.com ■ £££
Opulent, quirky and colourful hotel where guests are made to feel like visiting celebrities. Great cocktail bar and a central location.

Fingal
(MAP P1) ■ Alexandra Dock, Leith ■ (0131) 357 5000 ■ www.fingal.co.uk ■ £££
After a £5 million makeover, this former working vessel has been transformed into a luxurious floating hotel. Permanently moored next to the Royal Yacht Britannia, it features 23 gorgeous cabins. It is also close to Michelin-starred restaurants and hip bars, and only 20 minutes from the city centre.

Balmoral
MAP N2–3 ■ 1 Princes St ■ (0131) 556 2414 ■ www.roccofortehotels.com ■ £££
The most prestigious of Edinburgh's old-school hotels, right on Princes Street, sports two great restaurants – Michelin-starred Number One and Brasserie Prince by Alain Roux. The hotel also has a spa with a Finnish sauna.

The Chester Residence
MAP J3–4 ■ 9 Rothesay Pl ■ (0131) 226 2075 ■ www.chester-residence.com ■ £££
These gorgeous serviced apartments, featuring luxurious furnishings, are spread across a number of townhouses. Breakfast can be delivered to your room. For an experience like a film-star, opt for the Owners Residence that has a private cinema.

The Glasshouse
MAP P2 ■ 2 Greenside Pl, Leith Walk ■ (0131) 525 8200 ■ www.theglasshousehotel.co.uk ■ £££
A private rooftop garden crowns this crystal palace of contemporary design tucked beneath the classical monuments of Calton Hill. Impeccable service, good food and suites with walls of glass, allowing views across the Edinburgh rooftops to the Firth of Forth.

The Scotsman
MAP P3 ■ 20 North Bridge ■ (0131) 556 5565 ■ www.scotsmanhotel.co.uk ■ £££
Formerly home of The Scotsman newspaper, this solid building has been transformed into a stylish hotel, that has, bright rooms. Superbly situated, it looks north over the New Town. The Grand

Café, offers an all-day menu as well as afternoon tea.

The Witchery
MAP M4 ■ Castlehill ■ (0131) 225 5613 ■ www.thewitchery.com ■ £££
Champagne and cookies await each guest in this cocoon of romance. Bose sound systems and cable TV are the modern touches in the nine antique-filled, indulgent suites. It has an excellent restaurant, Witchery by the Castle (see p81).

Edinburgh's Boutique and Mid-Range Hotels

Malmaison Edinburgh City
MAP N2 ■ 21-22 St Andrew Square ■ (0131) 370 4600 ■ www.malmaison.com ■ ££
Conveniently located next to Edinburgh's main bus station and close to Waverley Station, this hotel features colourful and cosy rooms. It is also within walking distance of all the sights of the New and Old Town.

Village Hotel
MAP W4 ■ 7 Festival Gate, Pacific Drive ■ (0141) 375 9266 ■ www.villagehotels.co.uk ■ ££
This sleek glass-and steel monolith on the Clyde belies its name. Ultra-modern inside and out, it's anything but rustic, with facilities including an indoor pool. It's well located for access to the SSE Hydro arena, and the

special offers often make it great value for money.

The Bonham

MAP K3 ▪ 35 Drumsheugh Gardens ▪ (0131) 226 6050 ▪ www.thebonham. com ▪ ££

Created from three Victorian townhouses, The Bonham makes a chic and comfortable base. It has bold styling, with modern furnishings and a range of communication and entertainment devices (including fast internet and DVDs). The restaurant cuisine tilts towards modern European.

21212

MAP Q2 ▪ 3 Royal Terrace ▪ (0131) 523 1030 ▪ www. 21212restaurant.co.uk ▪ ££

Four luxurious rooms set above a fabulous Michelin-starred restaurant that offers contemporary French fare. Rooms have views of leafy gardens and are decorated in cocoa and caramel shades, with soft sofas and king-sized beds. Waverley Station and the sights of central Edinburgh are within a 10- to 20-minute walk.

Fraoch House

MAP F5 ▪ 66 Pilrig St ▪ (0131) 554 1353 ▪ www. fraochhouse.com ▪ ££

A lovely Victorian building whose period features have been fused with contemporary design to produce a clean and vibrant modern look. Delicious Scottish cooked breakfasts will set you up for a day of sightseeing.

Nira Caledonia

MAP L2 ▪ 6-10 Gloucester Place ▪ (0131) 225 2720 ▪ www.niracaledonia. com ▪ ££

Located off the beaten path in upscale, peaceful Stockbridge, Nira Caledonia is still within easy reach of the city centre. This is an elegant boutique cocoon, carved out of several adjoining Georgian townhouses, offering spacious and stylish rooms.

Market Street Hotel

MAP N3 ▪ 6 Market St ▪ (0131) 322 9229 ▪ www.marketstreethotel. com ▪ ££

This brand-new hotel is a one-minute walk from Waverley Station. Bedrooms are Scandi-chic in style, which combines minimalist design and functionality. The rooms are also larger than most in the Old Town area. The Nor' Loft café and champagne bar overlook the Scott Monument.

Malmaison

MAP K5 ▪ 1 Tower Pl, Leith ▪ (0131) 285 1478 ▪ www.malmaison. com ▪ ££

As its name suggests, Malmaison looks to France for inspiration, and provides a winning mix of good brasserie food and contemporary styling in its rooms – and wonderful bathrooms. Nicely set on the quay with all its restaurants.

Rabble

MAP M2 ▪ 55a Frederick St ▪ (0131) 622 7800 ▪ www.rabbleedinburgh. co.uk ▪ ££

You'll find very stylish rooms at Rabble, each kitted out with GHD hair straighteners and a fully-stocked Smeg fridge. Cooked breakfasts are served until noon, with takeaway bags available for those making an early start.

Edinburgh's B&Bs, Budget and Self-Catering

Castle Rock Hostel

MAP M4 ▪ 15 Johnston Terrace ▪ (0131) 225 9666 ▪ www.castlerock edinburgh.com ▪ £

Castle Rock is a lively, cheerful and well-run hostel in an excellent central location just off the Royal Mile and below Edinburgh Castle. The large common rooms have a piano and coal fire as well as free Wi-Fi. There is a sun deck that provides breathtaking city views. Amenities include a guest kitchen for self-caterers. In addition to large dorms, they also have quads, triples and doubles.

Brooks Hotel

MAP K5 ▪ 70 Grove St ▪ (0131) 228 2323 ▪ www.brooks edinburgh.com ▪ ££

Brooks is a reasonably priced, modern, bright and comfortable hotel, in a rustic stone building. In such a compact capital, none of the main sights are very far away, and either the Old Town or Princes Street can be reached within a 15-minute walk. All the rooms are fully equipped with TVs, decent beds, uncluttered decor and en-suite showers.

Georgian Apartments
MAP M2 ■ 26
Abercromby Place
■ (0131) 624 0084
■ www.georgian
apartmentsedinburgh.
co.uk ■ ££
For self-catering in
style, head to these
two properties in leafy
Abercromby Place
both have a double
bedroom, plus two
beds in a screened-
off section of the living
room, a fully equipped
kitchen, free Wi-Fi and
free parking. There is
a two-to three-night
booking policy.

Gerald's Place
MAP M1–2 ■ 21B
Abercromby Place
■ (0131) 558 7017 ■ www.
geraldsplace.com ■ ££
This B&B is situated in
the elegant Georgian
New Town. There are
just two bedrooms, each
with private bathrooms
and power showers.

Haymarket Hub Hotel
MAP J4 ■ 7 Clifton Terrace
■ (0131) 347 9700 ■ www.
haymarkethubhotel.
com ■ £
This smart budget chain
hotel in the West End is
located along the tram
route. The chain has con-
veniently located hotels
within walking distance of
Princes Street and close
to Haymarket Station.

Glasgow's Luxury Hotels

Sherbrooke Castle
MAP Y3 ■ 11 Sherbrooke
Ave ■ (0141) 427 4227
■ www.sherbrookecastle-
hotel.com ■ ££
A baronial building in a
quiet residential corner

of Glasgow close to
the Burrell Collection,
and an easy 10-minute
train ride from the
city centre. The decor
alternates between
an upbeat, boutique
look and a more tra-
ditional, somewhat
stately feel.

ABode Glasgow
MAP X3 ■ 129 Bath St
■ (0141) 221 6789
■ www.abodeglasgow.
co.uk ■ ££
A Neo-Classical
19th-century townhouse
has been given a designer
makeover, artfully blend-
ing Edwardian wood
panelling and ironwork
with a modern aesthetic
look. The rooms are
spacious, with big beds
and pillows you could
easily nest in.

Blythswood Square
MAP X3 ■ 11 Blythswood
Square ■ (0141) 248 8888
■ www.kimptonblyths
woodsquare.com ■ £££
This elegant boutique
hotel on a quiet central
Glasgow square features
marble interiors and
tweed furnishings. It
has a bustling restau-
rant, a popular bar
and a spa.

Hotel Du Vin
MAP Y2 ■ 1 Devonshire
Gardens, off Great
Western Rd ■ (0141)
378 0385 ■ www.hotel
duvin.com ■ £££
This stretch of Victorian
terrace in the West End is
the epitome of timeless,
sophisticated luxury.
The individually styled
rooms are awash with
deluxe fabrics and care-
fully selected antique
furniture. Enjoy opulent

bathrooms and
high-tech gadgetry
in the bedrooms.

Malmaison
MAP W3 ■ 278 West
George St ■ (0141)
378 0384 ■ www.
malmaison.com ■ £££
Malmaison exercises
its mantra of getting
the details right: large,
comfortable beds,
mood lighting and self-
indulgent bathrooms,
with power showers
and baths suitable
for hour-long soaks.
There's a French-style
brasserie in the crypt
(the building is a con-
verted church) and a
gym to counterbalance
all the lazing about.

Glasgow's Mid-Range and Boutique Hotels

Alexander Thomson Hotel
MAP X4 ■ 320 Argyle
St ■ (0141) 221 1152
■ www.alexander
thomsonhotel.co.uk ■ £
This modern hotel has
spotless contemporary
standard rooms. It is in
a convenient city centre
location close to Glasgow
Central railway station.

The Brunswick
MAP Y4 ■ 106–108
Brunswick St ■ (0141) 552
0001 ■ www.brunswick
hotel.co.uk ■ £
Housed in a smart,
copper-topped building
in the buzzing Merchant
City area, this hotel has
a modern-chic interior
that is not too formal
and a friendly café-bar.
The rooms are well-lit
with modern amenities
such as flatscreen TVs
and free Wi-Fi.

Novotel
MAP W3 ▪ 181 Pitt St ▪ (0141) 619 9001 ▪ www.all.accor.com ▪ £
While the Novotel is unlikely to feed the mind with recollections of a truly memorable stay, it does provide simple, comfortable accommodation with inoffensive decor. Food and drink are readily at hand in the pleasant bar and restaurant.

Apex City of Glasgow Hotel
MAP X3 ▪ 110 Bath St ▪ (0141) 319 4570 ▪ www.apexhotels.co.uk ▪ ££
Behind its curiously angular glass façade, the Apex offers superb value for money in a very central location. The spacious rooms have pristine facilities and boutique styling. All have Sky TV and free Wi-Fi.

Grasshoppers
MAP X4 ▪ 87 Union St ▪ (0141) 222 2666 ▪ www.grasshoppersglasgow.com ▪ ££
Located right above Glasgow Central train station, occupying the former Caledonian Railway Company building, this contemporary hotel offers sleek, Scandi-style rooms with pod-like bathrooms. It offers a cracking breakfast buffet too.

Glasgow's B&Bs, Budget and Self-Catering

Dreamhouse Apartments
(0845) 226 0232 ▪ www.dreamhouseapartments.com ▪ £
In various West End locations close to Kelingrove Park, these luxurious one- and two-bed apartments have modern styling and full maid service. An excellent choice if you're staying for more than a few nights.

Glasgow Youth Hostel
MAP Z2 ▪ 8 Park Terrace ▪ (0141) 332 3004 ▪ www.hostellingscotland.org ▪ £
Although it's half an hour's walk from the city centre, Glasgow's SYHA hostel enjoys a lovely setting in an elegant and spacious Victorian mansion overlooking Kelvingrove Park, convenient for Kelvingrove Art Gallery & Museum. Some of the rooms have glorious views.

CitizenM Glasgow
MAP X3 ▪ 60 Renfrew St ▪ (0203) 519 1111 ▪ www.citizenm.com ▪ ££
This Glasgow outpost of the CitizenM hotel chain offers compact, ergonomically designed rooms with en-suite bathrooms. It has a 24-hour self-service restaurant.

The Alamo Guest House
MAP Z2 ▪ 46 Gray St ▪ (0141) 339 2395 ▪ www.alamoguesthouse.com ▪ ££
Art, antiques and ornate original plasterwork lend a period atmosphere to this gorgeous 19th-century townhouse in a prime West End location, just a few minutes' walk from some of Glasgow's top restaurants. Perks include posh toiletries, bathrobes and a movie library, while the more expensive rooms have garden views; the best room has a luxurious freestanding bathtub.

Mainland: Luxury Hotels

Knockinaam Lodge, Portpatrick
MAP H3 ▪ Portpatrick ▪ (01776) 810 471 ▪ www.knockinaamlodge.com ▪ ££
Knockinaam nestles in a romantic setting by the sea. Room rates include top-quality dinner and breakfast (see p89).

Boath House, Moray
MAP D4 ▪ Auldearn, Nairn ▪ (01667) 454 896 ▪ www.boath-house.com ▪ £££
A Georgian mansion set amid gardens and woodland, this is not just a hotel but also a luxury retreat with a sauna, spa, gym, and a full range of beauty treatments, including Ayurvedic remedies. Good healthy food completes the package.

Cameron House, Loch Lomond
MAP F4 ▪ Nr Luss ▪ (01389) 310 777 ▪ www.cameronhouse.co.uk ▪ £££
An enduring favourite to which many stars hop by helicopter from Glasgow. Right on Loch Lomond this turreted mansion has extensive leisure facilities, including a large pool, tennis courts and a marina. At mealtimes, choose between the fine dining Boathouse restaurant, the Tamburrini and Wishart gourmet restaurant, and the golf-themed Clubhouse restaurant.

For a key to hotel price categories see p144

Culloden House, Inverness

MAP D4 ■ Culloden Rd, Balloch ■ (01463) 790 461 ■ www.culloden house.co.uk ■ £££

Bonnie Prince Charlie stayed here (he commandeered the place in 1746) and the hosts have dined out on the story ever since. Glistening chandeliers and Adams plasterwork enhance a building of exceptional architecture. Every room at Culloden House is uniquely decorated, and there's superb dining, too.

Glencoe House, Glencoe

MAP E3 ■ Glencoe ■ (01855) 811 179 ■ www.glencoe-house.com ■ £££

This lovely 19th-century mansion, built by the governor of Canada's Hudson Bay Company, still sports much finery from the time, including marble fireplaces, parquet floors and ornate ceilings. Service is attentive but not intrusive: breakfast is served whenever you want.

Gleneagles, Auchterarder

MAP F4 ■ Perthshire ■ (01764) 290 021 ■ www.gleneagles.com ■ £££

A superb country house resort, arguably Scotland's finest, with warm personal service and old-fashioned style. Leisure activities available at Gleneagles include cycling, riding, archery and a fantastic spa, not to mention a world-class golf course (see p57). The resort is also home to Scotland's only two-starred Michelin restaurant, the French-influenced Andrew Fairlie (see p95).

Inverlochy Castle, Fort William

MAP E3 ■ Torlundy ■ (01397) 702 177 ■ www.inverlochy castlehotel.com ■ £££

This has been among Scotland's elite for so long, it has become the benchmark for excellence. The hotel is set against a stunning landscape of surrounding mountains and has sumptuous decor. The King of Norway presented the dining-room furniture as a gift, and he wouldn't be disappointed with what's served upon it.

Isle of Eriska Hotel, Ledaig

MAP E3 ■ Benderloch, nr Oban ■ (01631) 720 371 ■ www.eriska-hotel.co.uk ■ £££

Isle of Eriska Hotel sees extravagant luxury on an island sanctuary near the mouth of Loch Linnhe. The hotel defines good living.

Kinloch House, Blairgowrie

MAP E5 ■ Blairgowrie ■ (01250) 884 237 ■ www.kinlochhouse.com ■ £££

With all the key features of a 19th-century Scottish country house, Kinloch House is the perfect place to experience the country's history. There are individually decorated rooms. Wander in the beautiful walled garden containing hundreds of roses, and explore the dignified public rooms including a venerable portrait gallery.

Mainland: Mid-Range and Boutique Hotels

2 Quail, Dornoch

MAP C4 ■ Castle St, Dornoch ■ (01862) 811 811 ■ www.2quail.com ■ ££

Exquisite little B&B offering three beautifully turned out rooms furnished in natural woods and tartan fabrics. You'll not find a better breakfast for miles around either.

Ednam House Hotel, Kelso

MAP G6 ■ Bridge St ■ (01573) 224 168 ■ www.ednamhouse. com ■ ££

Overlooking the River Tweed, this classic Georgian mansion is a major draw for its rooms as well as the restaurant. The building itself retains period features and makes for a comfortable base to explore the glorious and scenic countryside of the Borders.

Fauhope, Melrose

MAP G5 ■ Gattonside, Melrose ■ (01896) 823 184 ■ www.fauhope house.com ■ ££

Built in 1897, this secluded house gives enchanting views of the River Tweed and Eildon Hills. It is tastefully decorated and the staff display impeccable hospitality. You will find rich colours, antiques and a bottle of sherry in the rooms. For the sheer comfort and price, this ranks among the best in the Borders.

Glen Clova Hotel, Glen Clova
MAP E5 ■ Nr Kirriemuir ■ (01575) 550 350 ■ www. clova.com ■ ££
This excellent old hotel offers fine food, character and relaxation in spades, in the best of central Scotland's scenery. Ideally located for keen walkers, this establishment offers a wide choice of stylish rooms and tasty food prepared with local produce. It proves to be a perfect retreat for everyone.

Glenfinnan House Hotel, Glenfinnan
MAP E3 ■ Bridge St ■ (01397) 722 235 ■ www.glenfinnan house.com ■ ££
An imposing 18th-century pine-panelled stately home which overlooks Loch Shiel. Excellent value, the rooms vary in price according to the views. Glenfinnan House has good home cooking and a bar where folk musicians often gather.

Macdonald Aviemore Resort
MAP D4 ■ Aviemore, Inverness ■ (0344) 879 9152 ■ www.macdonald hotels.co.uk ■ ££
This resort, located in the highlands, has three hotels and 18 luxurious self-catering woodland lodges – so offering something for all budgets.

Old Pines Hotel, Spean Bridge
MAP E3 ■ (01397) 712 324 ■ www.oldpines. co.uk ■ ££
This Scandinavian-style hotel in a single-storey house, with easy wheel-chair access, has a play area for children and views to Ben Nevis. Dinner at the restaurant (see p121) can be included with accommodation rates.

Manor House, Oban
MAP E3 ■ Gallanach Rd ■ (01631) 566 429 ■ www. obanmanorhouse.com ■ ££
An outstanding place to stay in Oban, with cosy rooms, an excellent restaurant and fine views over the bustling harbour. The ferry terminal and railway station are a 10-minute walk from the front door, and there is free off-street parking.

The Seafield Arms, Cullen
MAP C5 ■ 17-19 Seafield St ■ (01542) 841604 ■ www.seafieldarmscullen. co.uk ■ ££
Re-opened in 2019 after a major makeover, this 19th-century inn offers accommodation in 16 stylish bedrooms with en-suite bathrooms. For families and groups, it offers spacious, modern cottage apartments with huge kitchens. It is a super stopover on the Moray coastal route to Speyside and Inverness.

The Newport, Newport-on-Tay
MAP E5 ■ 1 High St, Newport-on-Tay ■ (01382) 541 449 ■ www.thenew portrestaurant.co.uk ■ ££
This venerable hotel has been given a facelift by master chef Jamie Scott and has four bedrooms themed around different countries. The restaurant features modern Scottish dishes based on locally sourced meat, game and seafood. There are stunning sunset views to be enjoyed over the Firth of Tay to the Tay Bridge while relaxing at the in-house bar.

Cringletie House, Peebles
MAP G5 ■ Edinburgh Rd ■ (01721) 725 750 ■ www.cringletie.com ■ £££
Built in the mid-19th century on the site of a much older property, this charming house is set in its own grounds. Rooms are individually designed and there's also a converted cottage with a hot tub.

Mainland: Guesthouses and B&Bs

Fiorlin, Melrose
MAP G5 ■ Abbey St ■ (01896) 822 984 ■ www. melrosebedandbreakfast. co.uk ■ £
Close to the abbey and set inside its own walls in a quiet cul-de-sac, this B&B offers very comfortable self-contained accomodation, with shops and a number of restaurants nearby. The owners are especially attentive to the needs of their guests.

Glencoe Youth Hostel, Ballaculish
MAP E3 ■ (01855) 811 219 ■ www.hostelling scotland.org.uk ■ £
This quiet hostel is situated in one of the most spectacular glens in Scotland, on the door-step of some of the best year-round walking and climbing. Compare notes with other ramblers at the famous nearby Clachaig Inn, where the day's mountaineering tales are swapped every night.

Glenfinnan Sleeping Car, Glenfinnan
MAP E3 ■ Glenfinnan Station Museum ■ (01397) 722 295 ■ www.glenfinnan stationmuseum.co.uk ■ £

The most unusual beds in Scotland are to be found in a disused railway sleeping coach, which now stands at Glenfinnan Station Museum. It sleeps 10, and you can pay by the night or hire the whole wagon by the week. All-day light meals are served in an adjacent coach. All aboard!

Globe Inn, Aberdeen
MAP D6 ■ 13 North Silver St ■ (01224) 641 171 ■ www.the-globe-inn.com ■ £

The bedrooms a the Globe Inn are located above one of Aberdeen's best pubs, so this is not a place for early-to-bed guests, but the value and the central location – can't be beaten. Hearty breakfast will set you up for the day. Paid parking.

Rowardennan Youth Hostel, nr Drymen
MAP F4 ■ Rowardennan ■ (01360) 870 259 ■ www. hostellingscotland.org. uk ■ £

This is one of the busiest youth hostels in Scotland owing to its superb location, which is on the banks of Loch Lomond and also on the West Highland Way walking path *(see p52)*. Ben Lomond sweeps up at the back and at the front is a private beach. Rowardennan is very popular with families. Definitely book ahead.

Beach Cottage B&B, Inverness
MAP D4 ■ 3 Alturlie Point ■ (01463) 231 676 ■ www.beachcottage inverness.co.uk ■ £

It's not unusual to see dolphins swimming in the Moray Firth from this renovated 18th-century fisherman's cottage, and rooms have been designed to make the most of the stunning views.

Five Pilmour Place, St Andrews
MAP F5 ■ St Andrews, nr Old Course ■ 0447904 371191 ■ www.5pilmour place.com ■ ££

The best of a string of pleasant guesthouses by St Andrews' Old Course, the rooms here have a modern boutique feel, thanks to high-quality furnishings and various comforts. Guests can enjoy the walled garden. An excellent breakfast is included in the room rate.

Mackay's, Durness
MAP B4 ■ Sutherland ■ (01971) 511 202 ■ www. visitdurness.com ■ ££

This long-standing family-run hotel has smart wood-and-slate decor in its log-fired lounge, and stylishly decorated rooms. It's welcoming as well as immaculate, and enjoys wonderful views of the surrounding countryside.

Rua Reidh Lighthouse, Gairloch
MAP C3 ■ Melvaig, Gairloch ■ (01445) 771 263 ■ www.stayatalight house.co.uk ■ ££

Built in 1912 by a cousin of Robert Louis Stevenson, this idyllic lighthouse offers some magnificent views over the Minch to Skye and the Western Isles. Tidy guest rooms and a self-catering apartment available.

Easter Dunfallandy Country House, Pitlochry
MAP E4–5 ■ Perthshire ■ (01796) 474 031 ■ www. dunfallandy.co.uk ■ £££

In an idyllic location overlooking the Tummel Valley, this lovely property has a cottage accommodating six people and two en-suite rooms in the main house. Enjoy inexpensive rural living, where the day begins with a hearty Highland breakfast.

Island Accommodation

Berneray Youth Hostel, Berneray
MAP C1 ■ North Uist ■ (0845) 293 7373 ■ www.gatliff.org.uk ■ £

A charming thatched cottage, Berneray Youth Hostel provides somewhat simple accommodation in the most stunning location. Plus it's just four hops to the beach.

Lochranza Youth Hostel, Arran
MAP G3 ■ Lochranza ■ (01770) 830 631 ■ Closed Nov–Feb ■ www.hostelling scotland.org.uk ■ £

In a beautiful location below Arran's mountains, and close to the sea and an ancient castle, rests Lochranza Hostel. Secluded in a woodland garden, this old country house makes a great base for exploring the island. It is close to a bus route and has its own small shop.

Salen Hotel, Mull
MAP E2 ■ Salen, Aros
■ (01680) 300 324 ■ www.
salenhotelmull.co.uk ■ £
Centrally located and close
to Ben More, this informal
hotel offers comfortable
rooms and superb views.
The dining room offers
panoramic vistas, and
there are hearty dishes on
the menu. Pets welcome.

Ardhasaig House, Isle of Harris
MAP C2 ■ Ardhasaig
■ (01859) 502 500 ■ www.
ardhasaig.co.uk ■ ££
Set by one of the most
picturesque roads in the
isles, this 1904 house has
been completely refur-
bished, while retaining
certain period features.
With light decor, simple
furnishings and captivat-
ing views, this B&B is of
the highest calibre. There
is the option of a four-
course set menu for
dinner. A self-catering
cottage is also available.

Broad Bay House, Lewis
MAP B2 ■ Isle of Lewis
■ (01851) 820 990 ■ Closed
Nov–Feb ■ www.broad
bayhouse.co.uk ■ ££
Beautifully located beside
a sweeping sandy beach,
this guesthouse is only
a short drive north of
Stornoway. The contem-
porary rooms are styled in
natural wood, with a glut of
hi-tech facilities.

Busta House Hotel, Shetland
MAP A1 ■ Brae ■ (01806)
522 506 ■ www.busta
house.com ■ ££
A remote and peaceful
country house hotel, this
is one of the great get-
away-from-it-all retreats
in Scotland. Busta House

delivers first-class quality
in every respect and detail.
It also has self-catering
family cottages.

The Colonsay Hotel, Colonsay
MAP F2 ■ Isle of Colonsay
■ (01951) 200 316 ■ www.
colonsayholidays.co.uk
■ ££
This traditional inn, built
in 1750, has always been
the island's social centre
and often hosts live music.
Rooms are bright and sim-
ple, and guests can enjoy a
garden, terrace and library.
Curl up with a good book
and enjoy some fine sea
views over the neighbour-
ing island of Jura.

Glenegedale, Islay
MAP F2 ■ Isle of Islay,
Argyll ■ (01496) 300 400
■ www.glenegedalehouse.
co.uk ■ ££
Glenegedale is a classic
whitewashed Hebridean
house in a glorious setting
overlooking Laggan Bay
and the Irish coast. Every
room here has been indi-
vidually decorated and
there is a full range of
modern facilities and
quaint touches, such as
roaring peat fires in the
colder months. An Cuan,
run by the same owners,
is a self catering property
located nearby, with spectacular Laggan Bay views
from its elevated position.

Pennygate Lodge
MAP E2–3 ■ Craignure,
Mull ■ 01680 812 333
■ www.pennygatelodge.
scot ■ ££
A Georgian manse, set in
its own grounds, overlooking Craignure Bay. The
rooms are decorated with
antiques, fresh flowers
and artworks. Some also
offer a view of the sea.

Viewfield House, Skye
MAP D2 ■ Portree
■ (01478) 612 217
■ Closed mid-Oct–Mar
■ www.viewfieldhouse.
com ■ ££
A rambling building set
in 81,000 sq m (97,000 sq
yards) of woodland garden,
Viewfield House has been
a family house since the
early 19th century. Guests
are made very welcome
and, if they so wish, can
choose to dine together in
the Victorian dining room.

The Kirkwall Hotel, Kirkwall
MAP A5 ■ Harbour St,
Kirkwall ■ (01856) 872
232 ■ www.kirkwallhotel.
com ■ ££
This fine Victorian hotel
on the harbourside has
37 modern and spacious
en-suite bedrooms. It's
within walking distance
of St Magnus Cathedral
and the ruins of the medieval Bishop's Palace. The
restaurant offers the best
of Orkney's surf and turf,
while the Highland Park
Bar stocks more than a
hundred malt whiskies.

Flodigarry Country House, Skye
MAP C2 ■ Staffin, Isle of
Skye ■ (01470) 552 203
■ www.hotelintheskye.
co.uk ■ £££
Situated close to the sea
and below the Trotternish
Ridge stands this 19th-
century mansion, which
retains many period
features and a fireplace
that is lit in winter. The
views from the sunny
conservatory are mar-
vellous. Flodigarry
Country House is an
affordable retreat with
a growing, glowing rep-
utation for good food.

For a key to hotel price categories see p144

General Index

to main entries.

A

Abbeys and priories
  Arbroath Abbey 94
  Dryburgh Abbey 53, 87
  Dunfermline Abbey 91
  Inchmahome Priory 103
  Iona Abbey and Priory 70,
    123, 125
  Jedburgh Abbey 53
  Kelso Abbey 53
  Melrose Abbey 53, 86
Aberdeen 108, 111
Accommodation 143–51
Act of Union (1707) 38
Adam, Robert 11, 32, 32–3,
  40, 87
Aerial sightseeing 54
Aiden, St 28
Air travel 136
Alloway 7, 85
Ancient Egypt gallery
  (Kelvingrove) 21
Ancient Egypt Rediscovered
  (National Museum of
  Scotland) 18
Angus Glens 94
Anstruther 53, 91
Aonach Mor 28
Applecross 55, 120
Ardnamurchan 45, 118
Arduaine Gardens 49, 104
Argyle Battery (Edinburgh
  Castle) 12
Armadale (Skye) 7, 26
Armoury (Culzean Castle) 32
Arran 55, 71, 104, 126
Arthur's Seat (Edinburgh)
  15, 77
Atholl, Dukes of 41, 91
Auchindrain Township 106
Avant Armour, The
  (Kelvingrove) 21
Aviemore 34

B

B&Bs 143, 145, 147, 149–51
Ba', The (Kirkwall) 69
Bagpipes 42, 69
Baird, John Logie 43
Ballater 111
Balmoral 41, 110, 111
Banking 142
Bannockburn, Battle of 6,
  38, 91, 103
Barra 54, 125
Barrie, J M 39, 94
Bars and pubs
  Edinburgh 80
  Glasgow 101
  see also Restaurants
Beach Leisure Centre
  (Aberdeen) 61, 108
Beauly Firth 119
Bell, Alexander Graham 43
Ben Cruachan 46
Ben Hope 46
Ben Lomond 46

Ben Macdui 46
Ben Nevis 28, 46, 117
Ben Vorlich 46
Benbecula 126
Best-kept secrets 58–9
Bicycles (Riverside
  Museum) 22
Birnam Oak (Dunkeld) 67
Black, Joseph 39
Black Mount 31
Blackwell, Elizabeth 43
Blair Castle 41, 91
Blairgowrie 53
Boat trips
  ferries 55, 136–7
  Fingal's Cave (Staffa) 70
  Loch Lomond 103
  Loch Ness 29
  PS *Waverley* (Firth of
    Clyde) 55, 100
  SS *Sir Walter Scott* (Loch
    Katrine) 44, 105
Bonawe Historic Iron
  Furnace (Taynuilt) 106
Borders Abbeys Way 52
Borders Railway 54
Borders Rugby Sevens 69
Botanic Gardens (Glasgow)
  49, 67, 99
Botticelli, Sandro
  *Virgin Adoring the Sleeping
    Christ Child, The* 16
Breadalbane Mountains 46
Bridge of Allan 105
Bridgewater Loan, The 17
Brown, Lancelot "Capability"
  40
Buchaille Etive Mor 47
Buckie 110
Budget tips 67
Burns, Robert 7, 14, 39
  Burns Monument
    (Alloway) 84, 85
  Robert Burns Birthplace
    Museum (Alloway) 85
Burns An'A'That (Ayrshire)
  69
Bus travel 136, 138
Bute 104

C

Caerlaverock Castle 40, 88
Cafés see Restaurants
Cairngorms, The 11, **34–5**,
  55, 111
Caledonian Canal 29
Calgary Beach (Mull) 123,
  125
Callander 105
Callanais Standing Stones
  (Lewis) 71, 124
Calton Hill (Edinburgh) 6,
  72–3, 76
Camellia House (Culzean
  Castle) 33
Camera Obscura
  (Edinburgh) 15
Campbell, Clan 44, 46
Campbell, Lady Grace 104
Canna 124

Cannich 119
Cape Wrath 45, 129
Car rental 138
Carnoustie Championship
  Course 56
Cars, Wall of (Riverside
  Museum) 23
Castles and fortifications
  40–41
  Armadale Castle (Skye) 26
  Balfour Castle (Orkney)132
  Balmoral 41, 110, 111
  Blair Castle 41, 91
  Brodick Castle (Arran) 104
  Brodie Castle 112
  Caerlaverock Castle 40, 88
  Castle of Mey 129
  Castle Stalker 31
  Cawdor Castle 41, 111
  Corgarff Castle 111
  Craigievar Castle 112
  Crathes Castle 111, 112
  Culzean Castle 7, 11, **32–3**,
    40, 85
  Doune Castle 105, 106
  Drum Castle 111, 112
  Drumlanrig Castle 88
  Duart Castle (Mull) 123,
    125
  Dunnottar Castle 41, 109,
    114–15
  Dunrobin Castle 120
  Dunvegan Castle (Skye) 7,
    26
  Edinburgh Castle 10,
    12–13, 40, 75, 77
  Eilean Donan Castle 7, 41,
    118
  Floors Castle 88
  Fort George 29, 111
  Fyvie Castle 109
  Glamis Castle 40, 93
  Inverarary Castle 105
  Kilchurn Castle 44
  Kildrummy Castle 112
  Lauriston Castle
    (Edinburgh) 78
  Loch an Eilean castle 34
  Rothesay Castle (Bute) 104
  Stirling Castle 6, 40, 103,
    105
  Urquhart Castle 29, 45,
    117, 119
  see also Palaces; Stately
    homes
Cateran Trail 53
Cathedrals
  Dornoch Cathedral 120
  Elgin Cathedral 112
  Glasgow Cathedral 66, 97,
    99
  St Giles' Cathedral (High
    Kirk) (Edinburgh) 8–9,
    14, 66, 77, 78
  St Magnus Cathedral
    (Kirkwall) 130, 131
Cave, Sophie
  Floating Heads 21
Cawdor Castle 41, 111
Ceilidhs 43

Acknowledgments

This edition updated by

Contributor Robin Gauldie
Senior Editor Alison McGill
Senior Designer Vinita Venugopal
Project Editors Dipika Dasgupta, Rachel Laidler
Assistant Editor Riddhi Garg
Picture Research Administrator Vagisha Pushp
Picture Research Manager Taiyaba Khatoon
Publishing Assistant Halima Mohammed
Jacket Designer Jordan Lambley
Senior Cartographer Mohammad Hassan
Cartography Manager Suresh Kumar
DTP Designer Rohit Rojal
Senior Production Editor Jason Little
Production Controller Manjit Sihra
Deputy Editorial Manager Beverly Smart
Managing Editors Shikha Kulkarni,
Hollie Teague
Managing Art Editor Sarah Snelling
Senior Managing Art Editor Priyanka Thakur
Art Director Maxine Pedliham
Publishing Director Georgina Dee

DK would like to thank the following for their contribution to the previous editions:
Rebecca Ford, Helen Peters, Alastair Scott, Nikky Twyman, Christian Williams, Neil Wilson

The publisher would like to thank the following for their kind permission to reproduce their photographs:

Key: a-above; b-below/bottom; c-centre; f-far; l-left; r-right; t-top

4Corners: SIME/Olimpio Fantuz 4b.
Alamy Images: age fotostock/Gonzalo Azumendi 63tl; The Artchives 10cl; blickwinkel 7tr, 129fcr; Blue Gum Pictures 129fb; Mark Boulton 30bl; Douglas Carr 32cla, 56b, 107clb; David Chapman 130br; Derek Croucher 26cl; Ian G Dagnall 10bl, 116tl; Karen Debler 35cra; Dave Donaldson 69tr; eye35 67tr; D. G. Farquhar 119clb; Keith Fergus 28bl; FLPA 11br; Philip Game 98cla; Jeff Gilbert 19tr; Ross Gilmore 74tl; Dennis Hardley 30-1, 47t, 49bl, 110t, 124cla; Cath Harries 62b, Hemis fr/Rieger Bertrand 11cb, Hemis.fr/Gregory Gerault 118ca; Jan Holm 11tr; Holmes Garden Photos/Neil Holmes 92cb; imageBROKER/Jose Antonio Moreno Castellano 102tr; Imagestate Media Partners Limited - Impact Photos/Peter Thompson 27crb; Brian Jannsen 14t; John Peter Photography 35bl, 84tl, 86tl, 98b, 104-5; Kayroxby Image Scotland 15br; Look Die Bildagentur der Fotografen GmbH/Andreas Strauss 12br; Loop Images Ltd/Cath Evans 125tl; Vincent Lowe 131cl; Matthew Clarke 54t; Niall McDiarmid 67clb; John McKenna 54cb; olaradzikowska 53br; Paintin/ Scottish National Gallery *An Old Woman Cooking Eggs* (1618) by Diego Rodriguez de Silva y Velazquez, 16bl; Photoshot 128cra; Prisma Bildagentur AG 23crb; M Ramírez 20cr; Rolf Richardson 29bl; David Robertson 4clb; Seymour Rogansky 47br; Kay Roxby 21br; Iain Sarjeant

109br; Scottish Mainland 59clb; Duncan Shaw 46bl; Steve Allen Travel Photography 43bl; StockImages 103ca; Ivan Vdovin 66cb; Scottish Viewpoint 31tr; David Wall 70b; Paul White - North West Highland Scotland 117br; Allan Wright 109t.
Angus Council: 94c.
Atholl Estates: Stephen Farthing 41br; Paul Booth 91tr.
At the Sign of the Black Faced Sheep: 113tl.
AWL Images (Jon Arnold & John Warburton-Lee Photography): Hemis 50-1.
BrewDog Edinburgh: 80tr.
Bridgeman Images: Art Gallery and Museum, Kelvingrove, Glasgow/*Old Willie - The Village Worthy* (1886) Sir James Guthrie 20bl; © Culture and Sport Glasgow (Museums) 10crb (d); Private Collection/© Look and Learn 38cb.
Cairngorms National Park: 34bl.
City of Edinburgh Council: Alan Laughlin 78cla.
Cocoa Mountain: 133cr.
Corbis: Nathan Benn 32cb; Hemis/Christophe Boisvieux 45tl, 75br; Guido Cozzi 2tl, 8-9; JAI/ Fortunato Gatto 119tl, /Mark Sykes 97tr; Loop Images/Sebastien Wasek 46cla; Hans-Peter Merten 110-1; Andy Trowbridge 132cb; VIEW Pictures Ltd/Hufton + Crow 23bl.
Crannog Cruises and Restaurant: 121br.
Crown Copyright Reproduced Courtesy of Historic Scotland: Santiago Arribas Pena 10ca, 70tl, 88tl, 130t.
Cup Merchant City: 101cra.
Dreamstime.com: App555 11tl, 58br; Jennifer Barrow 11cra, 28-9, 75tl, 76b; Serge Bertasius 35tr; Lukas Blazek 4crb; John Braid 34-5; Bukki88 120tl; Tomáš Bureš 2tr, 36-7; Valeria Cantone 4cr; Richie Chan 26br; Cphotography 57t; Dbeatson 34crb Elxeneize 6cla, 24-5, 26-7; Eudaemon 66t; Nicola Ferrari 71ca; Paula Fisher 132tr; Georgesixth 77clb, Giuseppemasci 94bl; Grian12 99tl; Nataliya Hora 4t; Irinadobrohotova63 65tr; Julietphotography 22c, 76cra; Holger Karius 126b; Andrea La Corte 13tr; Emanuele Leoni 71ca; Lowsun 6ca, 117tl; Thomas Lukassek 44crb; Douglas Mackenzie 108tl; Magsellen 85tr; Daniel Masters 103b; James Mcquarrie 26cb; Meunierd 23c, 96tl; Jaroslav Moravcik 48t; Photographerlondon 55bl; Photoprofi30 66bl; Photovtch 124-5bl; Pitsch22 90tr; Adrian Pluskota 4cl; Juergen Schonnop 32-3; Stevewphoto 30br; Yvonne Stewart 103tr; Stockcube 4cla; Sueburtonphotography 123t; Petr Švec 12-3, 28cl; Tazufos 31clb; Tonythomas 1958 82-3; T.w. Van Urk 56cl; Stefano Valeri 91b; Andrew Ward 122br; Weetoonpics 122tl; Ketsiree Wongwan 19tl; Ian Woolcock 58t.
Edinburgh Festival Fringe Society: Jane Barlow 69cl.
Eilean Donan Castle: 41t.
Fife Coast and Countryside Trust: Richard Newton 53clb.
Getty Images: AFP/Andy Buchanan 39bl; Alan Copson 3tl, 72-3; Ross Gilmore 68tr; Hulton Fine Art Collection/National Galleries of Scotland 43tr; Loop Images/Universal Images Group/

Martin Berry 79tr; Maremagnum 3tr, 44-5, 134-5; Michael Breitung Photography 114-5; Oxford Science Archive/Print Collector 39cla; David C Tomlinson 15ca; WPA Pool/Robert Perry 39tr.

Glamis Castle: 42tl 93clb.

Go Ape: Red Consultancy 60tl.

Inveraray Castle: 105bl.

iStockphoto.com: YuriFineart 1.

Knockinaam Lodge: 65cl, 89br.

Landmark Forest Adventure Park: Captivating Photography/Charné Hawkes 61t.

Loch Lomond & The Trossachs National Park: 52t.

Mary Evans Picture Library: Illustration by J R Skelton in Scotland's Story (1906) 38tl.

Moonfish Cafe: 113c.

National Galleries Of Scotland: Van Gogh, Orchard in Blossom 17bl.

National Museums of Scotland: 18bc; Stewart Attwood 18cr.

National Trust for Scotland: Arduaine Garden 33cra; Kathy Collins 33bc; John Sinclair 32bl, 112bl.

Princes Square: 100br.

Scarista House: 127cra.

Scottish National Galleries: *Lady Agnew of Lochnaw* (1932) by John Singer Sargent 16tr.

Scottish National Gallery of Modern Art: 77tl.

Scottish Seabird Centre: 61cb.

Shutterstock.com: Ivica Drusany 106cla.

The Achiltibuie Garden Ltd: Allan Graham 49tr.

The Dome: 80bl.

The Kitchin: 81c.

The Peat Inn: Gill Mair 64cb, 95tr.

The Witchery by the Castle: 64t.

Cover images:

Front & spine: **iStockphoto.com:** YuriFineart.
Back: **123RF.com:** Jacek Nowak crb, stroop tl; **Dreamstime.com:** Leonid Andronov cla, Helen Hotson tr; **iStockphoto.com:** YuriFineart b.

Pull out map cover image:
iStockphoto.com: YuriFineart.

For further information see:
www.dkimages.com

Penguin
Random
House

First edition in 2003

Published in Great Britain by
Dorling Kindersley Limited
DK, One Embassy Gardens, 8 Viaduct
Gardens, London SW11 7BW, UK

The authorised representative in the EEA is
Dorling Kindersley Verlag GmbH. Arnulfstr.
124, 80636 Munich, Germany

Published in the United States by
DK Publishing, 1745 Broadway, 20th Floor,
New York, NY 10019, USA

Copyright © 2003, 2023 Dorling
Kindersley Limited
A Penguin Random House Company

23 24 25 10 9 8 7 6 5 4 3

A CIP catalogue record is available
from the British Library.

A catalogue record for this book is available
from the Library of Congress.

ISSN 1479-344X
ISBN 978-0-2416-1218-7

Printed and bound in Malaysia

www.dk.com

As a guide to abbreviations in visitor information blocks: **Adm** = admission charge; **D** = dinner.

MIX
Paper | Supporting
responsible forestry
FSC™ C018179

This book was made with Forest
Stewardship Council™ certified
paper – one small step in DK's
commitment to a sustainable future.
**For more information go to
www.dk.com/our-green-pledge**

Selected Street Index